Leading Learning Outdoors from Birth to Seven

This book reveals how early childhood leaders and practitioners can lead and enhance children's play, learning and experiences outdoors. It considers all aspects of outdoor provision from the importance of the setting's vision, routines, boundaries and expectations to the impact of staff and parental attitudes.

The book explores the benefits of the outdoor environment for children and how it benefits all areas of learning and development. Covering the role of the adult, the environment and resources at different ages and stages of development, the chapters offer practical guidance on creating high-quality outdoor play experiences for all children throughout the year. Kathryn Solly also addresses common barriers to outdoor learning and highlights the strategies that can be used to champion outdoor learning with colleagues, leaders and managers and children and their families.

Featuring rich case studies and photographs to illustrate good practice, this is essential reading for early years leaders, managers, educators and students.

Kathryn Solly is a retired headteacher of Chelsea Open Air Nursery School and Children's Centre. She is now an international Early Childhood speaker, consultant and trainer, as well the author of *Risk, Challenge and Adventure in the Early Years.*

Leading Learning Outdoors from Birth to Seven

A Guide to Philosophy, Pedagogy and Practice

Kathryn Solly

LONDON AND NEW YORK

Designed cover image: Kathryn Solly

First edition published 2026
by Routledge
4 Park Square, Milton Park, Abingdon, Oxon, OX14 4RN

and by Routledge
605 Third Avenue, New York, NY 10158

Routledge is an imprint of the Taylor & Francis Group, an informa business

ISBN: 978-1-138-34884-4 (hbk)
ISBN: 978-1-138-34885-1 (pbk)
ISBN: 978-0-429-43650-5 (ebk)

DOI: 10.4324/9780429436505

Typeset in Melior
by Apex CoVantage, LLC

Contents

Dedication and acknowledgements

This book has been a challenge. Health issues, the pandemic and other issues have really been dominant so it has taken far longer than expected.

I am so grateful to my family, KEYU colleagues (and their families) for the photos. I also thank the numerous educational leaders and champions who have contributed in different ways to make the book come alive with their outdoor leadership examples. Thanks particularly must go to my supportive husband George and my patient editor Annamarie.

This book is dedicated to our grandchildren: Emilia, Jack and Rhys. May you always value nature and learning outdoors and pass your passions on to your own children.

Introduction

This book is aimed at anyone working with young children who wishes to make a real and genuine difference to their play, learning and experiences outdoors. Outdoor play is the best way to support young children's learning and development when led well, but provision can be variable and there is often pressure for teaching and learning to be formal and structured. I argue that outdoor play provides essential developmental experiences that enhance children's learning in a way that cannot be done inside.

We will explore in depth the nature of outdoor leadership and reflect upon how adults should lead pedagogical practice. The importance of vision, ethos, routines, boundaries and expectations will be discussed alongside the why's, where's, when's and how's of leading child-led play-based learning outdoors. Throughout there is an emphasis on respect and collaboration to create a high-quality experience for all concerned – children, families and staff.

The chapters will encourage readers to reflect upon their roles and responsibilities when leading provision outside as well as the challenges and include practical strategies and real case studies to help link the theory to practice.

Chapter one sets the scene by outlining the main figures, philosophies and practices which have influenced outdoor leadership over the years.

In Chapter two we explore the theories of leadership and how these may differ for outdoor provision. It considers who are the outside leaders and what outdoor leadership looks like.

Chapter three looks at how outdoor play and learning are led in various countries including Scandinavia, Italy, New Zealand, Germany and Britain's 4 countries. It also examines the effect staff and parental attitudes, culture, behaviour and experiences have on outdoor provision.

Chapter four shows how leaders provide for high quality experiences and opportunities for babies and under threes outdoors alongside case studies from a variety of contexts. There is guidance on effective leadership approaches, staffing, the environment, partnership with parents as well as essential policies and procedures.

DOI: 10.4324/9780429436505-1

Outdoor learning for children aged 3–5 is the focus of Chapter five. We examine the role of the environment in supporting young children's development, play and learning and how this can be resourced effectively for this age group. There is also guidance on using the outdoors to enhance children's language and communication, physicality, and their health and wellbeing.

We next explore outdoor learning with 5–7-year-olds in primary schools and some of the leadership challenges this presents. Children often have fewer outdoor learning opportunities in school but benefit hugely from concrete play experiences that support self-regulation and how they take charge of their own learning.

In Chapter 7 we explore how our beliefs and values influence our leadership outside and the qualities that are central to being an outdoor leader.

The final chapter reflects on our collective responsibility in building and enhancing our connections with nature and ensuring children continue to have high quality outdoor learning experiences. It considers the role of community and how families and practitioners can work collaboratively to develop sustainable schools and settings that value the importance of nature and play.

No matter how small or large your outdoor space, I hope this book will help you to enhance your pedagogical practice for young children from birth to 7.

The present

Overview

For over two hundred years there have been competing views about early childhood which have influenced how it is viewed today. These include:

- The socialisation of the young child who is wild and free.
- The innocent young child who needs protection alongside reasonable freedom to develop and mature.
- The blank slate of 'tabula rasa' where child development occurs through the provision of critical foundations which will enable children to achieve their potential.
- The importance of interacting with nature to nurture and support child development enhancing children's potential and experience.

This chapter will consider the main figures, theories, approaches and philosophies which have been linked to leadership outdoors from the earliest days until the present time. These key pioneers have influenced our understanding of early years practice and leadership outdoors.

Starting with Comenius, we examine the how theories have developed over time and what we might learn from them to improve our leadership today.

John Amos Comenius (28 March 1592–15 November 1670)

As both a theologian and an educator, Comenius led schools and advised governments across Protestant Europe including England, Sweden and the Netherlands through the middle of the seventeenth century. Comenius was the innovator who first introduced pictorial textbooks in 1658: The 'Orbis Pictus,' written in the Czech language became the most renowned and the most widely circulated of school textbooks.

DOI: 10.4324/9780429436505-2

Comenius gave us:

- The basis of education as an agent for social change and equality of opportunity for all children. This is highly relevant to the rights of all children to play and learn outdoors as well as inside and establishes a foundation for outdoor leadership.
- An early example of how important innovative leadership is in early childhood and how it can be transferred across different countries. Comenius shows how we can learn from others in different contexts and cultures in terms of how we lead.
- Teaching based upon natural and gradual growth learning from simple to more complex concepts. This requires practitioners to have a rich understanding of child development and developmentally appropriate pedagogy and provision. So just like plants and animals which follow cycles of birth and development throughout life we need to provide education that understands and respects child development giving children time to develop at their unique pace.
- Life-long learning via education should one of the main areas of focus of the leaders.
- The value of logical thinking rather than dull memorisation.
- An opening for the education of women as well as the need today to encourage a far greater involvement of male role-models.

Jean-Jacques Rousseau (28 June 1712–2 July 1778)

Rousseau's philosophy is mainly focused upon developing character and moral understanding in order to live within an imperfect society. He became an advocate of developmentally appropriate education creating 3 simple phases of child development:

- Up to age 12 when emotions and impulses guide the child.
- Ages 12–16 when reasoning starts to emerge.
- Age 16+ when the child grows into an adult. For this stage he stresses the need to learn a craft and focuses upon process-based learning.

Rousseau gave us:

- The basis of developmentally appropriate education indoors and outside with that opportunity to be wild in nature and follow the lead of the children and their interests and fascinations.
- His child-centred ideas, which are credited as influencing such later pioneers as Pestalozzi, Montessori and Dewey, which in turn have influenced us.

Johann Heinrich Pestalozzi (January 12, 1746–February 17, 1827) Pestalozzi felt that education should be broken down into stages in order that children could fully understand. He also stressed that a child's personality, character and reasoning ability influenced how they would learn. This led to providing education that was child-centred and based upon unique differences, interests and ideas. He also recognised the numerous influences upon the child – their family, home, community, state and nation. Together with a colleague – Niederer, Pestalozzi was a significant influence on the importance of physical-education and outdoor activity linked to intellectual education.

Pestalozzi gave us:

- Child-centred education broken down into phases, providing for each unique individual, their interests, strengths and needs. This demonstrates to leaders that a strong foundation is based upon child development. It also shows how the outdoors can provide a natural and developmentally appropriate environment. This is seen in the Hadow Report in 1931, which stressed that the primary school curriculum should be based on the children's knowledge and experience, not on abstract generalisations or theoretical principles.
- An understanding of the joint influences of family, school and community recognised an important feature of genuine partnership with others who have a vested interest in what is provided for young children.
- A foundation for physical education, which underpins outdoor play and learning and is a key factor in why early childhood leaders celebrate high quality outdoor provision.

Robert Owen (14 May 1771–17 November 1858)

Owen was a Welsh textile industrialist whose advocacy, philanthropy and social reform ideals led ultimately to the creation of the trade unions and co-operative movement. He worked very hard to create decent working conditions and he established the 8-hour day in his factory in New Lanark, Scotland. He tried to support child labour laws and co-educational schools and built good relationships with his workers. Many of these workers had started as orphans from Glasgow aged 5–6 years old.

Owen believed people's good characters developed from their physical, moral and social influences from their earliest years.

He gave us:

- The first infant school with a focus on activity and play indoors and out.
- An understanding that early childhood should provide for babies and young children via a non-authoritarian leadership approach, which was healthy, content and educated indoors and outside.

- The model of leadership vision coalescing into practical provision and pedagogy.
- The inspiration for the provision of libraries, parks and schools.

Friedrich Froebel (21 April, 1782–21 June 1852)

Froebel invented the concept of the *kindergarten* (the garden of children) in Germany in 1840. His publication in 1844 of the Mother Songs emphasised his belief that women were capable of becoming teachers by extending their role in the home to educate children.

Froebel was the first pioneer to really see the full potential of the outdoor environment and its rich potential for learning. He also recognised that childhood is a phase in its own right. He saw that child development and the uniqueness in each child should be respected and valued. The kindergarten movement embedded the philosophy of the potential for play to integrate learning and development for the benefit of the child. He also recognised the connectedness of the child as a part of a family and a community and their unity with nature. Adults provide the supportive framework within these environments that scaffolds the child's development through 'freedom with guidance.'

Froebel recognised that children learn through activity and established the pedagogical concept that a child's work was play and therefore had educational value. He provided experiences such as singing, dancing, drawing, and self-directed play using the Froebel 'gifts' which were a carefully developed series of blocks and other simple objects for children to explore, play with and learn from. He also strongly encouraged exploration of the wider world around the children and took them to see local craftspeople and those working in agriculture and the community. Linked to these he developed the occupations for children to learn a wide variety of skills and competencies through construction, sewing, papercraft etc.

Froebel gave us:

- Quality nursery education as we know it today.
- The recognition that children need to be able to access and be in nature as a core principle and central focus for early childhood leaders.
- The concept that different experiences develop the whole child through the interconnected ideas of knowledge, beauty and form alongside the imagination, physicality and emotional experiences.
- The concept of wooden blocks as the resources 'the gifts' and the 'occupations' as workshop/zone-type experiences that are the basis of early childhood provision indoors and out.
- An understanding that childhood is a distinct phase of development which needs an approach which provides respect, and trust, alongside the scaffolding

of play by adults. This approach values integrated play, learning and child development and the space and opportunities offered naturally outdoors.

- The interconnectedness of child, family, school and community and how leaders must work in genuine partnership going at the pace of the unique child and their family whilst extending their learning of the world around them in the community.
- The means to develop the symbolic life of the child through music, movement, dance, song and rhyme as parts of the broad and deep curriculum.
- The close connection between child development and nature with the adult leader as the gardener to nurture the children with love and gentleness so they prosper and grow. In turn the children observe nature and gradually extend their knowledge through experiences outdoors and within the community.
- The concept that learning outdoors is deep and meaningful and it lasts throughout life for adults as well as children.

John Frederick Dewey (October 20, 1859–June 1, 1952) Dewey, an American, saw schools as places where social reform should take place as well as a means of educating citizens. He believed that children learnt best in an environment where they are allowed to experience, explore and interact with their own learning. Dewey's educational theories were presented in *My Pedagogic Creed* (1897), *The School and Society* (1900), *The Child and the Curriculum* (1902), *Democracy and Education* (1916) and *Experience and Education* (1938).

He believed the curriculum should be linked to experiences to help the child engage with the knowledge rather than purely about the subject matter to be taught. He became concerned about some of the proponents of 'child-centred' education and instead established experiential education or 'hands-on' learning.

Dewey gave us:

- The understanding that real-life experiences underpin children's learning.
- The crucial task of keeping alive a child's spark of wonder through real and active experiences.
- A vision of practitioners educated now and for the future and the need for high quality continuing professional development outdoors as well as inside.
- The idea that practitioners need to have a passion for knowledge and an intellectual curiosity for the materials and methods they use. This was central to how he saw the profession and leadership. This has a great bearing on staff selection and training as an outdoor leader's passion, knowledge, skills and understanding are crucial to them being confident and competent in their professional role.
- The awareness that the professional teaching career and leadership role would be very demanding.

Maria Montessori (August 31, 1870–May 6, 1952)

In 1906 Montessori was invited to oversee a project working with vulnerable children and families living in the slums of Rome, Italy. She was appointed as co-director of the Casa dei Bambini school which was for children aged 2–7 years, described in *The Montessori Method* in 1912 and in *The Discovery of the Child* in 1948.

The classroom was established with small tables and chairs, a blackboard and materials which Montessori developed herself. The activities included practical tasks such as personal care, dressing and undressing and care of the environment such as dusting, sweeping and gardening. She observed children's involvement and saw that when given free choice of activity, their concentration increased, and activities were often repeated as the child's sensitivity towards the environment was enhanced. This led to her increasing the choice of activities to also include gymnastics, handwashing clothes, pet care and cooking. In the large open-air classroom, Montessori encouraged the children to free-flow across all the activities as she realised that giving them autonomy enhanced their levels of understanding. Over time the children develop what Montessori called 'spontaneous discipline' by moving on to new and different challenging materials.

The Montessori method of education for young children stresses the development of a child's own initiative and natural abilities, especially through practical play indoors and out.

Montessori gave us:

- An environment which enabled young children to learn easily and via their own pace indoors and out through quality resources, experiences and opportunities to revisit time and time again. This is turn requires clear leadership and understanding of the ethos and principles of pedagogy especially outdoors.
- The view of the young child as a scientist in their approach to learning. This is a cornerstone of how outdoors provides the essential seedbed for young children's learning and should therefore be central to outdoor provision in all settings.
- The need for leaders to understand and value the importance of providing children with the opportunity to develop sensitivity to their environment; through the provision of activities and access to plants and pets;
- The understanding that children should be treated as individuals if they are to reach their full potential.

Patrick Geddes (2 October 1854–17 April 1932)

Geddes was a Scottish biologist, geographer, sociologist, philanthropist and town planner He was fascinated by Eastern philosophies 'to see life whole' to better understand human beings in their natural, social and built environments. He saw his role as two-part:

i) to provide ideas to allow people to adapt and improve their lives according to the opportunities and challenges of the places they lived,

ii) and to change the culture through education.

To do this he moved his family to live amongst the tenement homes of Edinburgh which in turn led to communal action via a clean-up and environmental improvement. He worked with architects using what he called 'conservative surgery' to retain and restore historic buildings whilst creating balconies and open courtyard garden spaces. By connecting ideas from different fields together he saw observation of any situation as the first step to changing and improving matters starting with improving the slums of Edinburgh and later Bombay and Jerusalem.

Gardens were an important facet of his social experiments and town planning initiatives and he believed that green spaces were essential for:

- Encouraging people to be active and outdoors.
- Producing local food.
- Improving the local environment.
- Enhancing community cohesion.
- Learning about bio-diversity, life forms, and the changing seasons.
- Taking responsibility and stewardship for the local environment.

In Edinburgh, as well as other cities, Geddes made use of disused and derelict spaces, however small, to create green spaces and gardens for the local inhabitants to tend and enjoy. He explored the philosophy of 'learning by doing' to find ways in which people could learn following this order of priority 'hand, heart and head.' This ecological approach of seeing 'life as a whole' is fundamental to the connections between leadership, nature and outdoor play which links to the ideas of Comenius and Froebel.

Geddes gave us:

- An understanding of the nursery garden as an important place to learn and to enjoy through the process of learning by doing. He recognised the important role that leaders have in ensuring this is provided especially for the most vulnerable.
- An awareness that the nursery garden needed rigorous outdoor leadership as it is a crucial area of provision for young children wherever you are in the world.
- The importance of growing food as a means of both feeding people and creating community cohesion from the young child onwards which has great parallels in our diverse society today.

- A vision that the education of children and adults is a cornerstone for ecological and social change especially in terms of biodiversity and caring for the environment. This underpins the whole concept of outdoor education in its widest sense.

Margaret McMillan (July 1860–27 March 1931) and Rachel McMillan (March 25 1859–March 25 1917)

The McMillan's philosophy was that children learned by exploring and would achieve their full potential through first-hand experience and active learning. They stressed the importance of free play, particularly with craft and water activities and also outdoor play – providing a large and varied garden for this.

Their school buildings described in her book *The Nursery School* (1919) were designed to face the south/south east and had a particular structure which linked to a butterfly formation with movable walls to let in as much light and ventilation as possible all year round.

The McMillan sisters gave us:

- The idea that a healthy environment is the basis of a healthy individual and can make a real difference to the vulnerable young child.
- The importance of free play and learning through exploration which can only really be provided outdoors.
- The basis of free school meals and the school nursing service.
- The importance of year-round access to outdoor play and learning for health and wellbeing in young children.

Grace Owen (1873–1965)

Owen followed on from the work of the McMillan sisters and pioneered family-orientated nursery schools with gardens being established in new housing development. She was principal of the Manchester Kindergarten Training College, recognised in 1917 by the Board of Education as an endorsed supplier of teacher training for children aged 3–6 years initiated by Margaret McMillan and later became the Organizing Secretary of the Manchester and Salford Council for Day Nurseries and Nursery Schools, and in 1920, she created a 'demonstration nursery school' at 61 Shakespeare Street, Manchester.

Owen and McMillan came from very different religious, political and social backgrounds and in later years were to disagree as to the methodology of training students in a divergence of views as to the importance of education and nurture within the nursery environment. This was during a period when nursery classes were developed in infant schools and McMillan saw it as the beginning of the 'schoolification' of early childhood.

Grace Owen gave us:

- The ongoing drive for Froebelian practice, leadership and teacher training indoors and outside in nursery provision in large inner cities.
- An awareness of the link between developmentally appropriate provision and how it is led indoors and outside.
- The establishment of family-orientated nursery provision again highlighting the need for genuine partnerships.

Susan Sutherland Isaacs (24 May 1885–12 October 1948)

Isaacs was an extraordinary teacher and one of the first to understand and question the work of Piaget. She published numerous books about her observations of young children's social and intellectual development seeing play as the central way for children to learn independence. Today we see children as competent learners who need warm relationships and enabling environments to support their exploration and play as a direct result of her powerful work and writing about the children at the Maltings School in Cambridge and lesser known as the guiding hand at Chelsea Open Air Nursery School, London.

Susan Isaacs gave us:

- The idea that the child's curiosity drives its motivation to learn through real-life opportunities with the outdoors feeding the curious minds of young children through awe and wonder.
- The central understanding that adults as outdoor leaders must strongly lead the vision, provision and daily pedagogical practice both inside and more so outside with the child's daily access to the riches of the garden and the rich opportunities in the local community.
- A huge appreciation of quality observation and need to observe children's play outdoors as well as inside in order to fully understand their learning;

Lady Allen of Hurtwood (10 May 1897–11 April 1976)

is known as a landscape architect and promoter of child welfare. As a campaigner for children in institutional care her work led to the passing of the Children Act 1948. She was also chairman (1942–1948) and president (1948–1951) of the Nursery School Association of Great Britain, founder president of the World Organisation for Early Childhood Education and a member of the Central Advisory Council for Education (1945–1949). After World War II she recognised the need for children to have play spaces within in their communities which were emerging as high-rise estates and led the development of outdoor adventure playgrounds in many British cities starting in war-damaged London.

She gave us:

- A re-awakened awareness of play and open-ended resources via adventure playgrounds. This links strongly with risk-taking, adventure, challenge and loose parts outside.
- An understanding that when the right conditions are provided, children themselves can take responsibility and gain leadership experiences. This is particularly true outdoors as the environment is more fluid and changeable.

Conclusion

Learning outdoors over time has concentrated on the 3 main domains of self, others and the natural world. The emphasis on these 3 areas have developed from these early pioneers and has led into the different approaches of the early childhood phase we recognise today.

Curiously, the approaches who still link in name to a philosophical founder such as Froebel and Montessori are more confident in both sharing and celebrating the roots of their practice and in providing it for children today indoors and out. The maintained nursery schools also have a very strong links back to the philosophy of the McMillan sisters and Isaacs which is evident in the high quality of their outdoor provision and pedagogy today. Holistically these all are centred on life skills such as problem solving, flexibility and adaptability, creativity and critical thinking, active learning, collaboration and team work, developing leadership skills and understanding of relationships, and the lasting value of nature and natural environments and resources to humankind. There are also strong links to being part of a community. The philosophies, ideas and approaches have germinated from around the world and from a variety of starting points. They all, however, reveal the crucial role of leadership in supporting outdoor play and learning for all children worldwide.

Grassroots leadership outside is an ongoing area for investment and needs particular focus in terms of distribution across networks, equity and inclusion as well as finding the best people to lead potential alliances and establish ways of working across the whole of early childhood. There is still a danger of a particular approach being seen as the saviour and single pathway for outdoor play and learning. 'One size fits few' so outdoor leadership requires clear vision clear modelling and continuous engagement with stakeholders via champions so that every family and community understand and value the crucial benefits from playing outdoors, management of daily provision, pedagogy and practice, real changes in policy, planning and procedures as well as sustainable funding. It also requires measurement of impact and further research as to long-term benefits in our fast-moving world.

2 What is outdoor leadership?

Introduction

Leadership can be defined in many ways depending on context, culture, competencies, values, processes, relationships and forms. This chapter considers some theories about leadership and how they apply to leading outdoors. It also reflects upon who are the leaders and what do they do both formally in terms of their roles and responsibilities and also in more informal capacities.

Defining early childhood leadership

Leadership theories

Before we discuss what leadership looks like outdoors, we need to consider what we mean by leadership in the early years. It is also helpful to highlight the difference between leadership and management. Geoff Southworth in several research papers about leadership in schools (1998, 1999, 2002a, 2002b) considers different kinds of educational leadership and some link to the areas of maintenance to management as:

> 'the process of causing to continue, keeping up, preserve.'

Whilst enhancement leadership is about:

> 'change, collaboration and improvement' as well as 'dynamic and interactive learning.'

This provides a useful starting point. Early childhood leaders and mangers can be responsible for a wide range of areas such as legal and financial administration, organisation, resource/time management, welfare and human resources. They are also responsible for offering high quality play experiences and learning built upon sound pedagogical foundations for the developmental phases of the children

DOI: 10.4324/9780429436505-3

involved. However, real leadership further requires individuals and teams to come together behind a shared vision and purpose as to how a setting works. This vision will encompass the welfare, pedagogy, practice and provision that is offered to the children that attend.

Southworth's *management (maintenance)* can be linked to Eden Charles's (1994) *'European perspectives'* which are linear and task orientated. This is akin to Judi Marshall's (1994): 'male' models which present as emphasising *separation, control, competition and focus in the same research*.

Further connections can also be drawn between *leadership (enhancement)* and the 'African/Asian perspectives' cited by Charles as *holistic, accepting, process and openness*. These ideas are taken further by theorists such as Formosinho, J. and Oliviera-Formosinho, J. (2012) who describe leadership as a *focus on philosophy and influence on relationships*. Whalley (2005) develops this further by suggesting that women as leaders use a *facilitating, community involvement style rather than authoritarian style* and are more concerned with influence rather than authority. Harries and Jones (2015, p. 152) takes this idea still further saying that:

> Future leadership will be concerned with participation and relationships rather than leadership skills, competencies or abilities. Future leaders will be spread across the organisation, and will constantly nurture and fuel new knowledge, new ways of knowing and new ways of doing.

This is central to leadership in early childhood which is driven by relationships, pedagogical understanding, empathy and professional skills and knowledge.

Who are the leaders in early childhood?

Heads and managers

In schools and early childhood settings the nominated leaders are those who ultimately hold the power and responsibility such as heads and managers. These have responsibility for establishing the vision and ethos of the establishment. This in turn is evident in how they lead, what they do and how they do it, with or apart from others. The pedagogical context indoors and out, the relationships and quality of what is provided for babies and children are a direct result of this vision and ethos. These are the figureheads who make or break the opportunities for outdoor play and learning. These professionals can be advocates and stand up for the child's right to be outside or they can go with the status quo and expect more formal learning inside.

Senior leadership team

There are also numerous other leaders who have crucial responsibilities within the setting/school with titles such as room leaders, senior leadership team, curriculum leader etc. In early childhood, any leader must be aware of the central importance of bringing the team together and creating a team of leaders who have a shared vision and purpose in providing the best possible education and care for young children. These leaders have defined roles and responsibilities which will help them prioritise their work as they lead their particular area of focus.

Informal outdoor leadership

Single figure positional leadership is a model which is increasingly seen as less useful in early childhood where the emphasis is on respectful and constructive relationships. Positive relationships are central to all the individuals involved whether they be children, families, staff or wider community. This has also been an embedded theme in documentation such as the *Early Years Foundation Stage: Statutory Framework* (Department for Education, 2008), the last *Children Act* (Department of Health, 1989); and *Every Child Matters* (Department for Education and Skills, 2004) legislation. This has resulted in shared and distributed models of leadership developing to allow more efficient use of skills, knowledge, relationships and expertise to break down tasks and achieve ends on finite budgets.

So finally, there are the softer/creative informal leaders who are understood by staff, parents and sometimes children to be natural, gentle influencers in particular areas such as outdoors. This may be an unrecognised role formally but that person will be the 'go to' person in particular circumstances for their knowledge, understanding and skills to assist when required. They are at ease and comfortable in their role and children and other adults recognise and value this strength. Such informal leaders express their strengths through an unseen process of *leadership within* and often encourage others to think differently by their support and engagement within the team. They are natural encouragers and support a positive culture of trusting, respectful relationships and interdependence. These informal leaders are also important influencers when team members express discontent. Such individuals are the people whom nominated leaders should carefully reflect upon as they may be the future role holders and leaders in the making.

All practitioners have the capacity to promote, protect and care for children's well-being and learning as a 'passion' (Moyles, 2001). Passion is often near the top of lists when thinking about leadership qualities in early childhood (Kaser & Halbert, 2009). Motivation to help and improve others is also extensively recorded as a driving force for individuals who would see themselves as quite humble practitioners. (Moyles, 2001; Rodd, 2006; Osgood, 2010). This powerful moral drive to care is clearly of central importance in early childhood professionals and helps them to face challenges, be active and make decisions to improve their practice. Again, this enables a broader participation and involvement in leadership and is far less dependent upon the nominated leader at the top.

Governors, management boards, trustees

There is also another tier of leadership which is often more external to the school or setting. Governors, management boards and trustee's involvement and understanding of the value, place and importance of outdoors can be extremely varied but hugely influential in positive or negative ways These community members and wider partnerships are essential as they can add a wider skill set and expertise to the staff and leadership team. Their co-operation can also add value to pedagogical practice, relationships and environments through shared values, understanding and interdependence as it is diffused out into the community. They can also add further reflective examples, role-models and connections to a learning/leadership-rich organisation and in building a learning community. This was a real blessing at Chelsea Open Air Nursery School where over the years we had several governors who were working or volunteering in charities, galleries, museums, gardens etc. They supported and extended the learning opportunities and curricular benefits for the children enormously by encouraging us to visit and use their skills and facilities.

Children and families

This community culture adds genuine value to the experiences for children and builds trust and positivity of diversity and inclusion whilst helping to resist conformity to conflicting external demands. Conflict turns into healthy debate and multiple perspectives are more likely to be voiced rather than driven underground to fester and cause harm. Ultimately the leadership role played by children in their choices, fascinations, genuine interests and involvement also plays a part in informal leadership. Trusting children to lead and guide us outdoors is very powerful but is about us respecting them in all of our work. This, sadly is getting harder because of the 'top down' pressure from political power and the economic expectation by society for settings and schools to fill more and more gaps in children's worlds.

What does outdoor leadership look like?

Leadership outdoors can be less obvious than that indoors. Some outdoor environments have physical cover for the adults, so they are far less visible than in an internal classroom situation. However, if there isn't leadership outdoors it is very evident in that the environment may be uninspiring or at worst borderline dangerous, the staff and children may be disenchanted and disengaged and the use limited, if never. Leaders should articulate, demonstrate and explain the key skills, knowledge and philosophy that underpin their setting's vision for children, particularly for the outside context as it is less predictable. Outdoor leadership can be evident in a variety of ways:

Figure 2.1 Let the child lead.

Articulating the key skills, knowledge and understanding

This is based upon the vision of the setting and its desire for children to experience and benefit from being in an outdoor environment, the quality of pedagogy provided and the rich opportunities available. This is evident in how staff are selected, appointed, inducted, trained and supported to provide the very best outdoors for the children. Areas such as policies and procedures, risk benefit assessment, first aid, food hygiene, clothing and footwear, access to outdoors, inclusion, SEND support and quality pedagogy will all underpin practices as parts of the vision. Where there is inexperience, quality continuing professional development will help ensure a sound foundation in each and every adult at different stages of their career.

Acting as a role-model to demonstrate the leader's role outside

Outdoor leaders 'walk the talk' by being, doing and getting down and dirty and genuinely getting involved outdoors with the children and team. This is how they establish their authority and commitment. Staff teams are quick to observe and judge those who say things but do not actually do them. They respond far more positively to those working alongside them experiencing the challenges and the benefits at least some of the time.

A leader will be outdoors with children and colleagues (as much as is feasible) as a role-model, an exemplar of learning and teaching within the outdoor enabling environment. The relationships they build will be strong, connected and rich with the children, families, colleagues and community over time as a result. They earn the respect they are given by doing the job of valuing and encouraging children's development and learning outdoors whilst putting in place the necessary policies and procedures to ensure their welfare and safety.

Valuing and understanding children's fascinations and needs

Leaders need to show that they value and understand children's unique developmental needs, motivations and fascinations. This means thinking about what is provided for children, how, when and where it is provided and placing value on the time given to engaging with the natural world. The outdoors should provide opportunities for adventure, risk and challenge and for meaningful learning across the whole curriculum. Some learning and experiences can only happen outdoors and each individual child should be able to follow their curiosity, access what they need to do and learn at their own pace.

A flexible and rich curriculum for each child

Every child is a unique learner. Any curricular provision must take this on board and allow for the staff to provide adaptable opportunities and experiences. Consider how language develops. The outdoors can add richness, variety and opportunity to support the development of new vocabulary and phrases. For example, a child who has never seen frost may squat down and melt the frost on blades of grass for a long time, whilst starting to understand the cause and effect their actions are having to melt the frost. A sensitive adult observing this can interact in an open-ended fashion to add to the child's experience.

Provide an optimum environment for learning

Leaders outdoors should maximise their space to enable effective, high quality outdoor experiences appropriate to the ages and stages of the children catered for. Environments outdoors for babies at different stages of development will clearly be

Figure 2.2 Helping adults with real life experiences ensures learning and different language opportunities.

very different to those for 5–6year-olds. For example, exploring mathematical concepts outside should be as large as possible via construction, tactile exploration, shape, measurement and mass. Leaders will maximise and extend possibilities, where appropriate, alongside the opportunities which occur naturally through children's play. Staff can interact to extend language, mathematics etc. suited to each child's developmental phase and interests. Outdoor leaders believe that the outdoor environment facilitates lifelong learning through rich play experiences and hands-on opportunities. This makes learning both real and meaningful and is clear in the *Statutory Early Years Framework* (DCSF, 2007):

> Outdoor learning is more effective when adults focus on what children need to be able to do rather than what children need to have. An approach that considers experiences rather than equipment places children at the centre of

> learning and ensures that individual children's learning and developmental needs are taken account of and met effectively.

The emphasis on children's experiences is clear and the outdoor leader should heed its focus of giving children time and opportunity to develop through their own experiences and not hanker after unnecessary equipment. The focus is on children being able to do things for themselves, to have genuine choices and being treated as unique individuals.

Balancing risk and safety

Children and parents need to have confidence and trust in those who lead, support and care for them too. Leaders need to manage risk benefit assessment, and encourage exploration whilst staying safe outdoors within nature. Some children/families may be anxious and wary so need time to build-up their confidence with this tricky learning. Outdoor leaders will also need to manage the environmental factors as much as is feasible. All the elements of care and welfare which are considered indoors will also need to be planned for outdoors but differently due to the unpredictability of the outdoor environment.

Recruitment and peer support

The provision of new outdoor-friendly staff will need carefully planned recruitment, induction, transition and ongoing continual professional development, often now with little or limited budget. These staff must come to know, understand and value that being outdoors and learning through play within it is fundamental. Often the best way is via role-modelling and buddying up to a champion who can sensitively steer and guide their emerging professional skills, knowledge and understanding of outdoors.

A definition of outdoor leadership

By drawing these ideas and elements together, I suggest that outdoor leadership can be defined as working together as a team with a common vision, purpose and pedagogy so that young children are provided with an optimum outdoor environment and education. This requires dynamic collaboration with all adults working together to improve and enhance outdoor learning and play by ensuring that the environment, practice and provision are developmentally appropriate. Each adult will provide different strengths and explorative opportunities to support this, whatever their starting point. Essentially, adults working together outdoors for the common good of children by starting with the child and their unique development.

Essential skills for all outdoor leaders

Any leader will need some essential skills to draw upon and guide the school/ setting towards its vision and purpose. The following are key:

- Clear vision.
- Confidence in being outdoors.
- High expectations.
- Deep understanding of pedagogy.
- Partnership working.
- Leading professional development.
- Building a culture of distributed leadership.
- Risk benefit assessment.
- Assertiveness.
- Sense of humour.
- Empowering others.
- Perseverance.
- Acceptance.
- Inspiration.
- Clear communication.
- Responsibility.
- Problem-solving.
- Accountability.
- Integrity.
- Honesty.
- Adaptability.
- Knowledge of their area/areas of responsibility.
- Reflection.

As role-models to young children and families, these are the professional skills, knowledge and understanding that anyone working or volunteering in early childhood should have or aspire to.

Leading change outdoors

Quality outdoor leadership is crucial if a setting/school really wishes to expand its outdoor provision for children. However small, such as a childminder's garden or large, such as school playing fields, your outdoor area needs a vision for outdoor learning which is paramount. This vision and plans linked to it will take time. It will be similar to a tapestry where a wide variety of items are added once the basic outline is established in coloured threads. It remains an ongoing process which at times will need to be unpicked and re-embroidered. The ultimate goal is to provide a rich, open-ended provision suited to the breadth of children and adults who will use it and which changes over time. It is a developmental process that will become embedded in the beliefs and values of the setting

Gaining support from co-workers

Beliefs and values about outdoors are embedded in us from our own childhood experiences. This was found by Ernst (2014) to have a positive correlation between the practitioner's beliefs about one's relationship with nature and the frequent use of outdoor learning environments. The most significant predictors of creating and achieving a successful outdoor environment were the real and perceived barriers and difficulties to using outdoors embedded in the practitioner. These barriers included lack of walking access, lack of time, weather, safety concerns and lack of extra supervision. Consistent with these findings, McClintic and Petty (2015) found that practitioner perceptions on the value of outdoor play, coupled with logistical constraints and curriculum demands, influence the use of outdoor learning environments in teaching and learning. In addition, the same researchers found that practitioners' 'minimal knowledge and skills of outdoor play environments, coupled with teachers' perceptions that indoor classroom learning is more important than outdoor learning' (p. 38) contributed to a disconnect between practitioners' appreciation of the value of outdoor learning and their actual practice as teachers.

Practitioners' strong beliefs and attitudes about outdoors are also unsurprisingly very much influenced by their own childhood experiences. Their knowledge of child development and how children learn through early childhood education, plus their own professional development are also crucial in how they see outdoors and appreciate its benefits. The anxieties and concerns about unfamiliar environments, potential hazards, space, strategic management of children's learning outdoors in gardens, play areas, playing fields and on trips and visits can be successfully supported collaboratively through modelling for both children and adults. This can ameliorate most anxieties and allow tentative exploration and emerging confidence. By engaging staff together collaboratively with children, families and colleagues as co-designers and users of outdoors, the negative anxieties start to dissipate gradually as everyone starts to understand calculated risk benefit, and other potential barriers.

There is also a vast need for high quality training and professional development outdoors as McClintic and Petty (2015) found. A lack of professional knowledge of and skills to use outdoors were also very influential in staff lacking confidence in the value and use of outdoors. The more staff understand the use of space, resources and time, the more able they are to face challenges and use and develop curricular potential to support child development alongside increasing their own exposure outdoors and within the local community.

Therefore, outdoor leaders need to stress a strong and consistent vision for all young children to access outdoor learning environments because:

- It is their legitimate right to experience and enjoy outdoors.
- Children thrive and prosper holistically through real experiences outdoors in terms of wellbeing, learning and development.
- Enthusiastic, well trained and knowledgeable adults are central to the children's experiences outdoors and will give the outdoor space equal status, time and value to indoors.

Beliefs and experiences are linked in the provision of outdoor learning and play as Ernst (2014) and McClintic and Petty (2015) demonstrate that once staff start to experience positive feelings themselves about outdoors, their attitudes change and children benefit. Staff should also be provided with adequate training, clothing, resources etc. in order to perform their role effectively and efficiently.

Senior management

There may be challenges from senior leaders and managers who don't understand, value or see the benefits of providing a rich outdoors environment for the children. This is where genuine belief and passion in outdoor play and learning can really make a difference. Reflection and personal confidence in the overall purpose and aims of what you are trying to achieve can bring about change via small and selective steps. It provides the motivation, determination and responsibility to act and make small but significant changes one at a time. Therefore, rather than dramatic wholesale change, it's worth exploring a small change such as the inclusion gradually of a few open-ended resources (loose parts) to an otherwise empty piece of tarmac and the commitment to interact and play with the children there. This will help others to see the environment differently and to start to understand its possibilities as the children become deeply engaged and behaviour issues decline.

Those in power will also see the practitioner's desire and willingness to persist and take responsibility whilst working actively to improve in order to make things better for children.

All these challenges alongside the equally draining apathy can be demotivating to practitioners who have been stopped or restricted by those above them. Some will express outrage at the suggestion that they should compromise their principles. In their book 'Leadership Mindsets: Innovation and Learning in the Transformation of Schools,' Kaser and Halbert (2009) theorise about *relational trust* as central to creating positive cultures and learning communities. This is where an outdoor leader can listen and take on board the ideas from the workforce and these are then seen as valued, considered and reflected upon by the nominated leader.

Appointing quality outdoor team members

Leadership outdoors takes numerous forms. The person who smiles, engages and interacts with children outdoors whatever the weather is highly likely to be a very desirable role-model. When appointing new staff members we need them to understand that the outdoors is highly valued and central to this setting/school. All interviewees should be pre-advised to come in their older work clothes as they will be observed playing with children indoors and out and need to be suitably dressed. Observing potential staff at play learning with children outdoors as a part of the interview process is critical. From my experience there are 2 reliable strategies which help.

- Firstly, offering a drink (hot or cold) in a sealed lid beaker. If the person walks around holding it close to them, it gets in the way of properly interacting with children. It can also give the unspoken message that it is more important than the interaction via body language to the child/children.
- Secondly, sending a child up to each candidate with a worm or similar. The candidate doesn't need to touch it, but engage and interact with the child about the minibeast.

At the interview stage these situations should be explained and discussed to gain the interviewee's perspective alongside providing a clear emphasis on the ethos of the setting and the expectations upon staff. This allows candidates to decide also if this is the job for them as well as avoiding mis-appointments. The setting/school should explain what support and provision it provides for its staff inside and out too e.g. clothing, footwear, training, flexibility and rotas.

The gentler, creative leaders are often the staff who are happiest outdoors. They may not have received much training and professional development to underpin their outdoor focus and fascination but with a small amount of support, encouragement and inspirational training they can fully transform into real outdoor ambassadors. Such specific outdoor Continuing Professional Development needs not to be that expensive as it can include visits to other settings, schools, gardens, museums; as well as suitable reading material, membership of useful online groups or courses/conferences etc. These adults have the innate attitudes and willingness to understand why outdoor play is essential for young children. Alongside these attitudes they are committed to young children and are positive in outlook which enables them to provide an outdoor learning environment in which children can prosper. These practitioners also recognise, capture and share the children's learning outdoors with parents and others so that they in turn understand, value and support outdoors via a cascade effect. These staff are often instinctively aware of cultural differences and attitudes towards outdoors. They generally know how to slowly and sensitively support and garner agreement with families to understand and value the realm of benefits and positive outcomes for young children outdoors. We need to further nurture and grow these outdoor ambassadors naturally as outdoor leaders.

Leadership within individual contexts and topology

Any outdoors environment is by nature very fluid and original. No two outdoor areas will be the same. There may be areas of natural provision as well as structural features which provide different opportunities. The environment ideally should provide areas, zones or bays for different kinds of experience e.g. gardening, construction, digging, climbing. The more appropriate the environment is for the children who access it and the more effectively it provides for open-ended choice and flexibility, then the greater the impact will be in meeting children's needs and interests, however large or small the actual space. Unique children may also need unique and personalised solutions for them to access, enjoy and benefit from being outdoors. This can be as basic as graduated slopes rather than steps; rails and handholds on steeper ramps; to special gear to keep a wheelchair user dry or braille to inform them about natural features which are nearby such as climbing boulders or a bird table for example.

The actual topology and geology of some sites can also make them very challenging. Narrow spaces alongside buildings limit viewing and often create undue shade so are far from ideal for growing. One of the most effective use of such a space I have seen was to create a hardstanding area for wheeled toys with road markings and resources. There were storage boxes alongside for ease of access to the toys and equipment.

Slopes can also be very problematical especially for children with limited physical skills. One setting used terracing on their site and built in a slide with steps and a slope into the bank. They also added a rope climbing area and raised gardening beds, providing great opportunities for their children and allowing children in wheelchairs some access too.

The surfaces of outdoor areas often cause much concern with mud being an issue in winter and dust in summer. I do not advocate plastic grass but rather more natural solutions such as involving the children in digging over the area, seeding it, caring for it before again being able to use it. Their involvement in the process is very valuable in engendering respect and understanding of their world. Short term solutions for mud can be wood chips or shavings or spraying the dust on windy days. Sometimes rerouting the pathways can help or actually laying a new pathway with the children using a variety of different materials and patterns.

Keep things open-ended if possible

The children playing and learning through their experiments with nature and raw materials now are tomorrow's engineers, designers, scientists, doctors, writers, philosophers etc. of the future. What, where and how they learn will influence their capacity to learn and grow in the future whatever their roles and responsibilities. What they play with must therefore provide the greatest affordances. The provision of plastic toys may have lots on initial attractions but a basket of cones, shells or log slices can provide ongoing enriching exploratory, imaginative and creative exploration and discovery. This has been supported by the work with loose parts/ open-ended resources of Froebel, Goldschmied, Nicholson and others. Compare the possible benefits of purpose-built structures with the endless possibilities of a den amongst tree trunks or a climb within its lower sturdy branches.

In deciding your ethos outdoors consider the following:

- The atmosphere or character of your outdoor area relating to the children who use it.
- The environment you have with fixed features and any possible obstacles such as trees, fences, sun and shade.
- The connections between indoors and out, for moving around in a variety of ways. Think carefully what kinds of storage you have and access to resources plus routeways in, around and out into the community.
- The constant presence of change in terms of weather, seasons, life cycles, children's needs and interests.
- Developing transition areas where outdoor clothing and footwear (for adults and children) can be managed. The provision of a covered area or zone is useful for this as well as other inviting experiences such as woodwork and large construction which may not have adequate space or sound proofing indoors. Reflect particularly on how babies can access and benefit from being outdoors in a variety of ways.
- The need to resource and provide open-ended resources for the children to use to understand space, shape, size, structure pattern, beauty and form through the introduction of planks, tyres, crates, logs and smaller natural items as props for child-led play and learning.
- Establishing an environment which allows adults to see/hear as much as possible whilst providing areas to be quiet, or spiritual.
- Ensuring the environment has rich opportunities for challenge by building in a level of risk through different heights, privacy, resources, movement, tools and rough and tumble play.

Figure 2.3 Puddle exploration.

- The provision and use of natural elements such as earth, water, air, sand, wood, metal plus, on occasions, fire.
- Ultimately reflect upon your outdoor area and whether it is a place to emerge, evolve and extend as a young child.

In summary effective outdoor leadership ensures

- A central focus on purpose, qualities and values rather than position and title.
- A focus on every children's unique development, learning and wellbeing and a shared understanding and aims of what should be provided for our youngest children especially those with individual needs.

- Children's rights, diversity and uniqueness are respected, valued and promoted appropriately especially for outdoors.
- A firm foundation of trust, nurture and unbiased relationships with children, families and communities.
- A rich culture of ethical study and analysis creating a community of learners.
- An understanding of and the sustainability of the natural world.

Reflection points

What is my role as a leader outdoors? What do I need to be particularly aware of?

There are innumerable things to consider as an outdoor leader but here are a few as starting points:

- What is our vision for outdoors?
- Which policies and procedures do we need? What about safeguarding?
- Whom and how do we appoint – practitioners etc.?
- Is out topology accessible? Is our communication inclusive?
- What resources do we need? Do we have a 'less is more' approach?
- What links do we have to with the community and potential cultural enhancement?
- Do we start with the child? Which essential skills do we teach outdoors?
- Do we enthuse and empower colleagues?
- Are we catalysts for change?

International and other models and their approach to outdoor leadership

Introduction

This chapter considers other models from around the world to outdoor learning and its all-important leadership. It will look at some tried and tested approaches which have influenced practice as well as the issues some practitioners face when leading outdoors in more challenging climates and conditions. Many of these approaches are based on the work of the earlier pioneers mentioned in Chapter one.

The forest/beach school origins and approaches

Sweden's Skogsmulle

Environmental education in Sweden began in the early twentieth century when the National School Plan of 1919 was mooted. It

> stressed the need for education in nature conservation and animal protection, in accordance with the social needs of the overwhelmingly rural, agrarian society of that time, and can legitimately be seen as forerunner to modern environmental education in Sweden.
>
> (Breiting & Wickenberg, 2010, p. 12)

The Forest School was first modelled on the open-air culture and Nordic philosophy 'friluftsliv' of Scandinavia and it emphasised the need to return to nature. It is a common part of life in Scandinavian countries, but relatively unknown to the rest of the world. In Sweden, the Forest School approach that we know today, has existed since the 1950s, when it was introduced by Goesta Frohm who created the idea of 'Skogsmulle.' Frohm felt that younger children were becoming removed from nature. To redress this situation, he set up a Skogsmulle school for children from 5 to 6 years of age. Like Froebel, McMillan and Isaacs before him, he believed

DOI: 10.4324/9780429436505-4

that first-hand sensory experiences outdoors, which included regular visits to the forest, would replace the stresses of modern life on children by reconnecting them with nature. His approach differed however, in that he executed this through an imaginary character called Skogsmulle (in Swedish *skog* means forest and *Mulle* is the name of a character who lives in a forest).

In 1986, the first 'I Ur och Skur' (in Rain or Shine) nursery opened and this led to a movement that resulted in over 190 nurseries and 20 primary schools based upon Skogsmulle pedagogy being established in Sweden. There is a clear progression from babies onwards of well-thought out and planned outdoor experiences, which reflects developmental need and age. Developmental empathy about understanding the world and its challenges is taught through the fantasy figure of Skogsmulle from around the age of 7. Children are simultaneously taught a range of outdoor sports such as skating, skiing and sledging too. Adolescents get to go on organised adventures and expeditions.

The Danish way

The first recorded Danish nature school is in 1950, when a woman called Ella Flatau formed a 'walking kindergarten.' This was a daily walk in the woods as a part of daily pedagogy. As congestion increased in Copenhagen, parents started to take their children by bus out into the countryside. The use of the outdoors for learning in Denmark grew from Froebel's pedagogy of child-centred education in natural environments.

Each 'forest school' setting in Denmark is unique wherever it is situated and according to those who are using it. The leadership structures again rather flat and democratic. Some, situated in woodland are usually called forest or nature kindergartens. These environments provide the focus for experiences indoors and out for a major part of the day, all year round. Most of these settings are small, with between 20–30 children and 4–5 practitioners. A few may take over 100 children.

'Forest groups' are also common in Denmark. These are clusters of children and carers who go out of their setting for part or the whole of the week to a woodland area. They often travel by bus and usually have a permanent or semi-permanent shelter as their base in the woods. A few too far away from wooded areas rent allotments and use that for their outdoor environment.

English forest schools

In England the movement towards Forest Schools probably originated with the creation of outdoor education centres in the 1940s. These grew from the Scouting movement (established in 1907) and the Woodcraft Folk (established 1924). The Plowden Report in 1967 provided the start of child-centred practice with no formal curriculum which linked up to the adventure playground movement of the 1970s. Increasing awareness of children's rights and the establishment of Rural and Environmental Studies alongside Field Studies as qualifications from the mid 1970s then provided teachers who were trained to teach children about nature and the world around them. I was one of them.

The Forest School initiative in the UK resulted from a visit in the early 1990s by a group of educators from Bridgewater College in Somerset on a visit to Denmark. They witnessed how the values of open-air living were embedded within the education system. On their return to Somerset, the educators established a B-Tech qualification for Forest School practitioners via structured training. This has remained the gold standard in forest school leadership ever since. Then various local authorities in England, notably Oxfordshire and Worcestershire took up the training of Forest School and worked with local colleges to deliver training. Others followed suit from Wales, Shropshire, Norfolk and Warwickshire. Finally, the Open College Network with the support of the Forestry Commission in Wales developed the ONC qualification in 2003. Today the Forest School Association has many members and this network has established some key features of Forest School:

- It is run frequently and regularly in a wooded or natural area, preferably throughout the year and aims to introduce children to new experiences and opportunities.
- It is led and run by qualified accredited level 3 practitioners who continuously maintain and develop their professional practice.
- It aims to promote the holistic development of all those involved, fostering resilient, confident, independent and creative learners by providing time and freedom to explore their own environment.
- It follows a child-centred pedagogy where children learn about and manage risks appropriate to the environment and themselves whilst gaining a sense of belonging, respect, understanding and value of the world around them.
- It has a high adult:child ratio.
- Observations of the learners are key to enabling scaffolding and planning of the learning and links closely to the revised *Statutory Framework for the Early Years Foundation Stage* (Department for Education, 2012).

Many of the activities are not restricted to forest sites but were suitable for smaller more limited urban areas too. These include the following:

- Build and cook on an open fire.
- Create a nest for a bird.
- Create dens, shelters, bridges and sculptures.
- Collect colours from nature.

- Mark-making experiences using natural materials.
- Create an assault course for a squirrel.
- Hunt for minibeasts in trees, bushes, deadwood etc.
- Create a bug hotel.
- Plant trees, lay hedges, maintain ponds.
- Climb trees.
- Listen to the heartbeat of trees (sap-rising).
- Examine the shape, scent, sound and surface of various trees.

A 2-phase evaluation project looking at the impact of Forest School on young children was undertaken in Wales and England from 2002 to 2005 through a partnership between Forest Research and the New Economics Foundation (O'Brien & Murray, 2007). It was used to track changes in 24 children at 3 case study areas over an 8-month period. The research highlighted that the children benefitted in a range of ways showing positive impacts in terms of confidence, social skills, language and communication, motivation and concentration, physical skills and knowledge and understanding. The wider impacts of Forest School on staff, parents, and the extended family also provided positive data. The Forest School approach provides an important opportunity for children to gain access to and become familiar with woodlands on a regular basis, while learning academic and practical skills. Crucially it also allows children to make meaning from their direct experiences if well led.

Beach schools

Beach schools are another valuable environmental area of pedagogy outdoors. These are also expanding as another locally based open-ended environment to provide holistic development and learning outdoors. They share the same aspirations and values as forest schools but through exploration of the varied ecosystems of beaches around our island. Children are encouraged to be physically active, forage, collect, be creative and imaginative, to take risks and explore possible challenges through problem solving. Developing an awareness of tides, water safety and weather is far more than just theory. Again, this is lifelong learning about nature and its potential hazards for us. Beach schools are learner-centred and give children a real opportunity to connect with sand, pebbles, shells, water, tides, and mud as well as a habitat for plants and animals whilst learning to respect, understand and value nature.

The training again has a strong pedagogical focus of weaving knowledge and practice together. Consider the huge range of possibilities from running free in a wide-open space, rock pooling, exploring oozing mud, dune jumping, climbing

Figure 3.1 Simple resources lead to fascinations.

and rolling, cooking marshmallows on a small open fire, making collections of shells and pebbles through sifting and sorting, creating stick pictures or dens with driftwood . . . as well as the tried and tested sandcastle building, kite flying, and mark making. The holistic development across social, emotional, physical and cognitive areas of learning are potentially vast. The children able to experience such opportunities move onwards in their learning because individually they are in a natural zone of proximal development. The adults who work with them understand leadership and risk benefit assessment and teach the children how to do things with reasonable safety therefore extending rather than restricting their learning about leadership and life.

The present situation

Increasingly Forest School provision is being set up within many schools and settings as headteachers and managers recognise the academic pressure being put on young children and the need to lessen it. For many it is an opportunity to offer a different way of learning and for children to engage in hands-on, self-directed skills learning including negotiation, resilience and independence outside. However, Liz Lightfoot in the Guardian (25.06.2019) reported that there are increasing concerns that the term 'forest school' has become a marketing gimmick giving legitimacy to the main focus on testing and assessment driven targets. Doing anything outdoors including bringing worksheets and even desks outdoors led to false claims about forest school simply because it is outdoors! This is due to a lack of understanding about the ethos and principles of forest school. It should immerse children in being outdoors, by learning new skills, having new and challenging experiences and following their curiosity. It is not about indoor practices being used outdoors as a classroom extension. Others criticise the forest school approach as too didactic and structured. This may result from whosoever is charge as much as the forest school ethos. Forest school appears to be a common 'buzz' word which some schools and settings are using to draw in families who wish their child to experience learning outdoors. In some circumstances this has led to a diluting of the ethos. This results from those who try to provide activities to tick off curricular outcomes rather than allowing children to freely play, experiment, explore, build relationships and be creative outdoors.

Forest and bush schools around the world

Forest schooling is gaining traction across the world. In **Canada** children are encouraged to interact with nature in age-appropriate ways; to develop and learn socially and emotionally; to be physically active; to develop self-confidence; to become self-sufficient; to work as part of a team; to explore and respect their locality and the world beyond. The child's role as a leader is very evident despite the environments being potentially more hazardous with wild bears and wolves nearby.

In **Australia**, forest or 'bush school' or 'kindy' as it is usually described, has grown as a direct result of the negative effects of societal pressure to get children 'school ready.' The development took longer to establish in terms of leadership and actual practice due to the research required to check out Australian flora and fauna with many poisonous snakes and spiders being a far greater health and safety issue than in Europe. Fire legislation is also very different too. It has led to a range of nature play clubs and experiences for children with their families too.

So, who is a forest/beach school leader?

Forest and beach school leaders have many qualities, but above all they

- Are passionate about being outdoors in nature and learning alongside children.
- Are intuitive and flexible, sensing change in learners because they work with them over long periods of time. They recognise trigger points, stress, misunderstanding, challenge, critical relationships and boredom in each unique child.

- Use the seasons to support learning and planning in time with children and nature.
- Have a thorough knowledge of child development, neuro-science, educational theory, safety and risk and therapeutic play. A deep understanding and knowledge of nature, environments and risk benefit assessment also underpin the role.
- Have a sound grasp of skills such as fire lighting, carving, using tools and knots etc.
- Know how to use close observation, reflection and analysis to enhance or develop experiences for each child's maximum benefit.

Coastal beach leader case study

Leah is both forest and beach school trained and has visited settings in Denmark in 2019 with Jane Williams-Siegfredsen who was part of the original team who went to Denmark from Bridgewater in 1993. Leah describes forest/beach schools as:

> not a survival course for children and they are not expected to take something home at the end of each session, except hopefully, a love of outdoors, new skills and abundant self-esteem. . . . The course changed the way I viewed teaching and subsequently led me to qualify as a Forest School leader in 2010.

As she lives near and teaches close to the coastline this teacher has grown up and raised her family with a love and respect for this environment. However, she is very aware that some of the children she teaches have never been to the beach. The Coastal School training she attended in 2019 was run by Essex Wildlife Trust and is an extension of the Forest School concept. She believes that 'how a child learns is just as important as what a child learns' So it makes sense 'to access the positive and challenging environment that is our local community as unique learning environments.'

Leah is also very aware of how the environment itself can limit the extent in which forest/beach skills are taught due to weather, litter and other factors. Her opinion is that 'risk' and 'health and safety' are the perceptions of the setting and society. Before the children leave a school/setting they are learning aspects of understanding the world and personal, social and emotional development in their planned visits as well as personal safety, for example, crossing roads, stranger danger, hygiene etc. An in-depth understanding of risk not just in the physical sense but also in terms of emotional development underpins her practice. Increasing children's confidence, promoting freedom and independence and controlled decision-making all enhance their self-regulation and resilience and perseverance. She is very well versed in standard practice of risk benefit assessing sites, establishing site boundaries and rules with children. She states that 'being able to connect with nature is the most powerful connection we have.'

Forest school leader case study

Sarah states that the Forest School leader's role is multi-faceted and includes 'relationships/team coach, learning mentor, H&S consultant, ecologist, logistics expert.' She states that 'their most useful tools are their ears and eyes as observation is key to trusting the children. Children know what they need to learn and generally know how to learn it.'

'The leader needs to be available to them, be aware of their emotional state and join them as they explore the world around them.' She is aware that every child is unique and no one responds in exactly the same way. 'A muddy puddle which delights one person may cause stress and anxiety to another.'

When discussing her own leadership journey Sarah mentions her first experiences of outdoor learning with Sybil Marshall author of *An Experiment in Education*. Children (20 boys and 5 girls) were her next teachers on a residential trip where 'We played, laughed, chased, rolled and sighed together.' This fed a desire from the children, staff and parents to discover, plan and fundraise to explore the natural world further through gardening, fishing, painting, singing and dancing outside! Parents became volunteers and this led to a week of community learning. A class of 'unteachables' had become 'within reachables.' Nature and playing together changed the story they were telling themselves. 'We discovered David loved to lie on his back and painted beautiful skies, Ronnie loved spiders, Tasha's greatest love was watching bees and butterflies visiting flowers under our classroom window.'

After this monumental start Sarah's experiences of teaching were far from her ideal until she trained as a Forest School leader at the Oxfordshire Forest School Project. She again witnessed the amazing change in children who would initially struggle to leave parents at the start of the day and yet would not stop talking on the way home in the minibus.

Sara helped the children remember their experiences in Forest School and apply them to other challenges.

> The weepy mathematician would be gently reminded of the time he was struggling to get a fire lit, 'How did you learn to do that?' something in his mind would shift and the lights would come on. He saw himself as a learner, not a failure.

She has gone on to design early years training and quality improvement at the Forest School Association. Her professional involvement with the Institute for Outdoor Learning (IOL) has also enhanced her broad understanding of leadership within the outdoor learning world. Due to the breadth of professional involvement the IOL from youth workers to teachers, nursery nurses to instructors they established a professional continuing development framework with its own language, accreditation and qualifications systems. The aim was to give the Forest School leaders a professional qualification, a means of progression and the respect due.

Sarah has also widened her connections and advocacy role by working with colleagues at the Sylva Foundation to create a sustainable, diverse and inclusive community of leaders. This moved Sarah to working with Forest School practitioners, landowners and conservationists to advocate the Sylva My Forest for Education woodland management tool which helps to address forestry sustainability issues whilst lessening eco anxiety. She is now a director of the Forest School Association and is further developing her coaching skills. Her view of early years colleagues on the FS training course is that they are 'the true heroes; they have taught their peers the value of observation, play and scaffolding learning. (through their training) They have also realised that how they have been taught themselves, throughout their lives has left them feeling "less than others."' She is very aware of the many issues which still restrict the leadership of learning outdoors in early childhood and sees these as:

- Early years dominated by women – limited role-models for boys.
- Lack of diverse role-models.
- The risk averse culture.
- The need for team coaching.
- Rural schools and settings having less access to nature because of being driven everywhere, no safe paths to walk on or close neighbours to play out with.
- Urban, inner city schools and settings often echo the determination of the pioneers in providing nature and freedom outdoors.
- Shrinking budgets.
- The need post-Covid for a Green recovery tax for a nature premium funded by tax or fuel similar to the Sports premium funded by the sugar tax.

New Zealand's outdoor approach

Since the Education Act 1989, school principals may give permission for children to attend alternative education outside the regular school premises, one day a week. This is known as One Day School. This is aimed at complementing the school curriculum and is aimed at children aged from 5–12 years. Holiday clubs for the same age group and adventure therapy provision for 13- to 18-year-olds are also available following the same forest school principles.

Roskill South Kindergarten

For younger children outdoor opportunities have developed slowly despite the outdoors playing a large part in the New Zealand way of life. Roskill South

Figure 3.2 Large sandpits are highly beneficial.

kindergarten started to explore 'bush kindergarten' as a trial it in 2009 using a reserve of native tress backing onto their premises. They knew very quickly it was providing the children with another environment to explore and learn through their play despite being in the city of Auckland. The bush kindergarten has now been running for 7 years and was initially limited to older children, one morning a week. In 2014 Roskill South adopted a day kindergarten model, and the programme expanded to include all children, and it takes place every afternoon, in addition to the Friday morning.

It provides an environment for the children to strengthen their dispositions and become highly motivated, self-directed learners who can make and lead their own plans and challenges with a special focus on risk-taking, self-management and building confidence.

Ngahere Tamariki at Discovery Kindergarten

In late 2015, Amy Robinson a teacher at Discovery Kindergarten in Whitby, near Porirua initiated Ngahere Tamariki – Children of the Forest – which sees the oldest children head into the bush near the kindergarten for 2 hours every week with one teacher and one parent helper. The programme focuses on encouraging children to become guardians of the environment. They learn to respect the flora and fauna and keep the area free from litter.

Similar to the European model the children at bush kindergarten go out in wet weather but they avoid thunderstorms and high winds. The projects have also benefitted from being part of the research project on Educational Leadership led by Wendy Lee. There is growing support for increasing nature discovery and bush kindergartens around New Zealand as it provides a wider range of learning environments and curriculum experiences. There is also a desire to provide 'wilder' experiences following a large interest in environmental sustainability.

Reggio Emilio outdoors

When visiting some of the nurseries of Reggio in 2006 in during the month of May I was rather disappointed that limited use was made of the outdoor areas at that time of year despite it being sunny and quite warm to the English visitors. This was due to the Italians being concerned about respiratory health and children were not encouraged to play outdoors until the weather was warmer. Different cultural attitudes towards weather plus health and safety both indoors and out are highly influential in terms of access and provision, for example, in allowing young children to access and use sharp tools far earlier than say in England, whereas the Italians are more protective of young children in colder, damp weather than we are. However, in Reggio I witnessed rich and exemplary use made of the learning potential of local community to follow and nurture child-led interests.

Reggio Emilia was founded by Loris Malaguzzi after World War I and is based around the educational philosophy that children, the environment and the teacher interact and each play a part in learning. Malaguzzi wanted the outdoor piazza to be a classroom without a roof as a multi-sensory place for children to use with freedom to choose when, how and why regardless of weather and time restraints. The children were to express their learning in hundreds of different languages (ways). The central pedagogical role of community involves 3 protagonists: children, educators and parents, who generate educational projects through shared values. The settings mirror the city with its central piazza and design with both the city and each setting being a workshop for exploration. It is this broader community which provides another powerful place to learn about the real world through a powerful learning community of inquiry.

The exploration of places and spaces indoors and out is based upon 'senses' and what is happening outdoors from weather, to seasonal change, from time of day to the rhythms of life. Often there are creative installations in light-filled rooms and courtyards that demonstrate the behaviour of physical forces such as wind, water etc. There are different scales and loose parts (open-ended resources) which are available for physical, social, exploratory, creative and imaginative play. This often includes sand play, a tinkering area or a sensory kitchen. There are always calm, quiet places for rest and reflection too. There is an interweaving of colour, light, sound, smell, architecture, design, and tactile which add dimensions to children's experiences. The settings provide safe but personalised spaces indoors and out which respond to the needs and interests of the children. The teams work democratically again with a relatively flat hierarchy. They follow a very powerful research-based philosophy where everything is reflected upon from the floor to the furniture; from open spaces for groups to child-like nooks to hide in all enabling sensory experiences and opportunities for child-led learning and development.

Working in less hospitable areas

There are many places around the world where teachers and practitioners are leading outdoor play and learning in far more challenging circumstances. These challenges include funding, political and religious controls and climate. The latter is an increasing issue as it is often also accompanied by pollution. In England extremes of cold, heat, drought, wind, rain, ice and snow are still highly unusual and usually limited to a few days a year. Nature elsewhere can also provide immense challenges too in the form of earthquakes, volcanic eruptions and similar disastrous scenarios. Huge restrictions can also result from religious, political or very severe economic constraints. Leadership outdoors within these challenging conditions and situations is crucially important and we can learn from it too. Many parts of the world are affected by typhoons, hurricanes and extreme winds and the resultant floods etc. The meteorological services try to protect people by issuing warnings in advance but climate change is making this an increasing challenge. In extreme situations the severity may cause so much damage and destruction that schools may be unusable or they become temporary accommodation for families displaced from their homes. Bodies such as UNICEF are now working to educate schools and communities so things return to normal as soon as possible for the good of the children. Schools and settings have established procedures which children and families are aware of and practice to prevent harm.

In China the government distributes advice each day as to the weather and pollution levels in 23 cities in order that the children stay safe. Readings of the tiny poisonous PM2.5 particles reached into the high 600s micrograms per cubic meter through the capital, as compared with the World Health Organization safe level of 25. Some Beijing suburban neighbourhoods logged levels up in the 900s in the winter months of 2015–16. Schools and nurseries were closed during a red alert whilst roads, air transport and many factories were closed or severely restricted as a direct result for several days. The government has tightened emissions standards and are investing in solar, wind and other renewable energy but the country still depends on coal for more than 60% of its power. Such toxic smog was recorded in England in the 1940s and 50s whilst other countries such as Poland (2017) and Bangkok (2019) have experienced similar issues with atmospheric pollution over recent years too.

China case study – *Hangzhou:* This bilingual setting has an established Outdoor Champion who is leading the development of the large outdoor free-flow space in a hot wet climate. The private school is one year old so is still in the development stage but has much to celebrate in their child-centred approach through an emergent curriculum and project planning. They have some open-ended materials and have established storage. The school also uses the Leuven scales so it is easy to measure the impact in terms of action research and second language acquisition. The Outdoor Champion has had to work extremely hard to achieve what has occurred outside as there have been several senior leadership departures. However, he is keen to discuss with the team and plan the layout, resources and learning so that it really caters to all children's interests and needs by offering what cannot be provided indoors.

The outdoor context

Each individual classroom has access to the outdoor area outside their room which is organised with a sheltered area leading out to the outdoors. Provision includes: planters, water, sand, and a big construction area which includes tyres, planks and pipes. There is also a bike track and wheeled vehicles. Further away from the classrooms is the mud kitchen/digging area. The latter was achieved by the Champion who took 3 days of his own time to dig out the mud pit. Seeing the children swarm to it creating volcanoes, restaurants and rivers has been the exciting reward.

Coverage and provision

The 2- to 3-year-olds find water play a major interest and this primarily tends to be sensorial experiences and activities arranged by teachers. The large outdoor area doesn't yet cater to all their needs especially in terms of their gross-motor development.

The 3- to 4-year-olds often seek engagement with the teachers. They are explorative and enjoy ball games and other projectiles but they engage for longer when with a teacher.

The 4- to 7-year-olds enjoy an equal share of the large construction, mud area and the bike track. These offer a range of experiences complimenting gross-motor development, creative initiative and often, teamwork.

Areas for development

The development of the Outdoor Champion role is really sound but that person needs to have coaching skills in order to enable the further development of the whole team in the move to maximise the use of this potentially rich outdoor area.

Children can find the space challenging in finding their place and direction within it. It is also a big area for staff to manage preventing them from getting 'involved.' There are resources of the fixed-kind such as a climbing frame which is apparently a legal obligation, however it is not massively used by the children so some creative reflection on developing this would be worthwhile. Water play is still an area for development overall. Water is generally drunk at least tepid for health reasons so this may provide a way forward.

Staff engagement is an area for real focus as the staff need guidance on how to interact with children outside which is often an issue worldwide. Many find the weather is a real challenge as they wish to be cool and dry and thus wish to work in the shaded/sheltered area rather than in the sun and rain. The weather can cause havoc with potential plans outdoors too. Not every child wishes to be out there when it is very hot, wet or cold and this is made worse sometimes by a lack of adult role-models. Staff do not like getting wet, hot and sweaty despite having good outdoor work clothes. Some really struggle with how to engage with the children when outdoors in areas where they haven't learnt how to enable play. Experience in the mud kitchen, with the blocks and bikes have increased engagement and confidence through training experiences. It is the spaces in between that they struggle with. The children who are not interested in those experiences also lose out as a direct result.

Parental views

Parents really struggle to understand the value of outdoors. They just see bad weather, coats, the inconvenience of washing clothes and their children getting ill as hindrances in their lives. Culturally outdoors is seen as a beautiful, aesthetically pleasing and 'entertaining' area for children, missing the pedagogical intricacies of what learning is possible and its potential for children.

Other challenges from weather

Many Asian and Middle Eastern countries also have to manage the effects of dust or sand storms. Countries as far apart such as Pakistan, South Korea, Taiwan and Kuwait may experience up to a third of the school year being affected by either sand or dust storms. Similar to atmospheric pollution such storms can affect the respiratory systems of children, the elderly or unwell and can sometimes pick up pollutants as well, making them doubly dangerous leading to asthma and pulmonary diseases as well.

Middle East case study

A large international school provides my case study for what I will call my 'desert school.' School provision outdoors in such areas of the world has its own unique challenges. The building is designed to allow ease of access indoors and out as an oval structure. Children have free access to the outdoor environment all day with generous staffing of 3 adults in each class of 20 children. So, depending on where the children are learning the adults in the class place themselves accordingly. There is no rota, the adults follow the children's interests and look out for potential hot spots to help facilitate learning. There is 1 member of staff who leads on Outdoor Learning and will share ideas during staff meetings to ensure that it is a collective responsibility a) to use the area effectively and b) to develop the children's social, emotional and physical needs. The school follows the EYFS and is keen to celebrate the progress in the children's general confidence, their social and emotional development, imagination, physical skills and risk taking which they often do not get at home or the rich opportunities for unstructured play. Features such as the mud kitchen for the younger children aged 3–4 years and climbing/balancing structures and large-scale construction for the 4–7-year-olds. Parents generally love the outdoors with a few worries about children getting hurt. Once they understand the ethos they really value it. The main challenges are:

- The weather, there are some months where it is simply too hot to use the outdoor environment.
- Contact with nature. E.g. Grass doesn't grow, thus ended up laying artificial grass.
- Resources need replacing regularly due to the hot weather.
- Ensuring all staff members understand and engage with the outdoor environment – team responsibility as well understanding how to facilitate the equipment for both Nursery and Reception children.
- The responder feels that a designated staff member who is solely in charge of outdoor provision, planning, organising, supporting staff development and running desert school would be advantageous.

Challenges of cold

Countries which are towards the north or south polar regions have other challenges – ice, snow and blizzards. In Britain and the USA there are no national or professional standards for temperatures that adults can consult when considering whether to keep children indoors. More often than not it is more an issue of the failure of internal heating, lack of staffing due to transport difficulties or external wind chill which leads to closures. The Education (School Premises) Regulations Act, passed in 1999, lays out the rules for teachers and school staff in England. It states that all school buildings must have a heating system to warm the rooms to the appropriate temperature. When the temperature is –1°C or below outside the school, they must be able to achieve the below temperatures at a height of 0.5 m above floor level. The Workplace (Health, Safety and Welfare) Regulations (1992) suggests that the minimum temperature in a workplace should normally be at least 16°C.

However, in many parts of Scandinavia, Russia and Canada children are allowed to play and even sleep outside at temperatures far below this.

Scottish nature kindergartens

The Scottish government has worked hard to develop 'Out to Play': Practical guidance for creating outdoor play experiences in early learning and childcare (2019). Whilst recognising the barriers to playing and learning outdoors in nature, it has joined forces with the Care Inspectorate to create a document not just for schools but also early childhood settings, childminders and out of school provision to use local green spaces. Its vision is centred upon the United Nations Rights of the Child Article 31(1) by wanting all of Scotland's children to have the best possible start in life through access to outdoor play-based learning every day. A coalition of 50 organisations and individuals came together to be part of the movement.

The document guides practitioners through the following areas:

- Finding the right outdoor space.
- Creating your space.
- Using your space.
- Staffing.

It moves from permissions to use land to establishing forest kindergartens alongside guidance on how to visit and use local green spaces fluidly through weekly or more frequent visits. It is centred upon wellbeing and generosity of spirit as well as GIRFEC – getting it right for every child. The philosophy is one of thinking big but taking small steps and builds upon Swedish, Welsh and Korean models. It is designed to be delivered outdoors by trained practitioners who can assess and check sites and understand children, weather, safeguarding, different environments, hygiene, risk benefit assessment and learning by adding value with things that cannot be man-made. The approach does not compartmentalise learning but sees it as holistic childhood experience and processes of engagement. The Scottish Government sees outdoor early childhood provision as a 'defining feature of childhood in Scotland' and has pledged more than £860,000 in 2018 to encourage and support greater use of outdoor learning in the early years across 8 local authorities. (the *Sunday Post* 30 July 2019). To see such practice in action it is well worth visiting: Secret Garden Outdoor Nursery https://secretgardenoutdoor-nursery.co.uk/

CASE STUDY: STRAMASH SOCIAL ENTERPRISE NURSERY

Stramash Social Enterprise Nursery operates for 50 weeks a year from a field which backs onto local Forestry Commission woodland.The service operates from their base at Spynie village hall, car park and field as well as a woodland site a short distance away by mini bus. The village hall and yurt on the woodland site provide warmth and shelter and an indoor space for the children if needed. There are places for a maximum of 32 × 2–5-year-olds in term time and 32 × 2–7-year-olds on school holidays. They have established an outdoor access code agreement to allow the mixed age group of children aged 2–5 years of age to play as freely as possible within this outdoor environment. It is recorded as providing a very good standard of day care by the Scottish Care Commission. Practitioners are observers and supporters as well as modellers. Children learn through their play and are supported to develop skills to risk assess their environment and play, for their own (and each other's) safety and comfort – physical and emotional. When the weather deteriorates the focus is on keeping children happy in their play but also warm and dry. There is a strong sense of community and older children being encouraged to lead and assist younger ones.

The ethos that is central outdoors is based upon

- Freedom
- Resilience
- Awe and wonder.

Leaders have observed that different ages often prefer certain areas

- 2–3-year-olds: Sand, water, mud and general exploration across the areas.
- 3–4-year-olds: Climbing, swinging and physicality, rough and tumble play. Collecting resources in the autumn and exploring in the spring and summer months.
- 4–7-year olds: Tool use, cooking, loose parts, exploration and collective challenges.

The main issues outdoors include:

- The perception that learning isn't happening; the children are messing around; children are feral or they won't be ready for school.
- Precipitation – Scotland can be very wet and cold.
- Proving that outdoor play and learning is the way forward and thus the approach of forest kindergarten doesn't fit into the established ways of recording, monitoring. Likewise, Local Authority expectations do not always fit with the Stramash approach.

Leaders have found the most rewarding aspects of their ethos as:

- Seeing the team develop and learn alongside the children with their confidence spreads to the children.
- Building relationships and sharing passions with other schools and nurseries, although there are very few like ours at present.

More troublesome areas for leaders include:

- Everyone accepting responsibility for overall safety and wellbeing as you cannot go on a course and suddenly know how, why, where, when and what do it across all areas with your children. . . . It's a learning process for everyone.

- Younger children's self-motivation to learn in very cold weather is inclined to evaporate so they need more adult-led activities and experiences. The older ones are more inclined to establish collective challenges. In warmer weather all the children can easily learn through their independent play.
- Some adults find it challenging to learn to let go of some aspects of controlling children and their spontaneous play in a variety of weathers. This can be daunting for those who are used to structured pedagogy.
- Getting the balance right between interacting or interfering and taking over the play leading to play paralysis.
- Finding settings with a similar approach for staff training visits to widen experience and reflection.
- Some parents have struggled with the lack of planning ahead and the choice being given to the children. They may ask 'What are they doing today?' and then receive the explanation that it's up to the children. This is improving over time through experience.

In these settings the collective reflective vision of the leader, the staff team, the children and families, the natural environment, the weather and the season are all very powerful informers of the provision and curriculum outdoors. The belief and confidence of the leader and staff in the approach is critical. If children are underestimated and not allowed to challenge themselves due to restrictive and tight boundaries, then no one flourishes. The move towards a nature-based kindergarten approach can mean considerable pedagogical change. For example: getting rid of a lot of resources or making practitioners aware that they cannot do the tasks that we want children to take part in such as cooking and fire preparation.

Learning is central to everything that happens and it happens without adult input too. The environment is also viewed as the teacher and is more natural and developmentally friendly to unique children in its approach as a result. Sometimes new developments such as woodwork take months of discussion and planning. The learning in this setting is all about experimenting with what works for children and staff.

Community driven projects

The Forest Schools as an international model has led to some creative and unique outdoor developments in Britain as direct spin off but in ways that really provide for local communities. They are led by a range of passionate individuals with a clear vision who have spawned a range of nature/nurture settings. These might be for young children in parks and local community areas often in large cities and cosmopolitan areas. Or they might be community inspired to save and maximise wild areas for the whole community.

I have witnessed the nature nursery approaches in 3 of such settings in London, Glasgow and Liverpool:

Little Forest Folk is London's first full-time EYFS immersive nature nursery established in 6 venues in Barnes, Chiswick, Fulham, Twickenham, Wandsworth and Wimbledon.

It is led by the vision of Leanna Barrett. Each nursery has been graded as outstanding in all areas and the accolades for leadership and management and safety are positive and clear. This is an organisation which strives through its excellent leadership to provide the very best teaching and learning outside for all its children. They are also a social enterprise and use some their profits to provide full-time free places beyond the government allowance to eligible children. Leanna is very aware that in times of change leadership needs to be robust and visionary 'where we try to constantly remind our teams of our ethos, our vision and what we are achieving in the world for our lucky children.' She remarked on the challenges for team leaders in last summer's heat. 'Leaders had to tread the fine line between assuring their teams that of course they could manage the heat, whilst also listening to and reacting to their requests and suggestion of how we could manage the heat better.'

Having opened 6 new settings in 4 years Little Forest Folk has now, having established a lot of credibility and a clear leadership and management structure, decided to establish an outdoor primary school – Liberty Woodland School. This venture has reminded Leanna of how leadership style has to change and adapt particularly in the early days when it needs to be far more hands-on.

> You have to lead, with confidence, on every tiny aspect of the outdoor learning. I will need to Head the school whilst teaching alongside my team all day, every day and working with them to ensure we are delivering the vision of primary school education we believe children deserve.

Nature to Nurture in Liverpool is another award-winning research social enterprise setting working collaboratively with Liverpool Hope University for the last 2 years. Their profits are used to educate students from Hope, Edge Hill and John Moores Universities. It is led by the passion and research of Julie White. They have developed an inclusive provision where children feel loved, safe and secure with attachment theory forming the basis of all they provide. Children experience a range of sensory and physical opportunities on a sessional basis which enhance emotional and cognitive learning through hands-on, joyful play and learning in a natural environment. Their ethos is about nurturing children in nature rather than following a forest school approach.

North Kelvin Wood and Children's Meadow, Glasgow

Finally, another approach can be seen in the city of Glasgow where Emily Cutts has led her local community in North Kelvin Meadow to change what was waste ground into an oasis rather than a housing development. Emily was driven to protect what she calls her 'Dear Wild Place' through a campaign for the Children's Wood and the Meadow. She understood the importance of nature and its proximity to people for their health and wellbeing and enlisted research support from the Psychology Department at Glasgow University. Her strategy was to get everyone involved going outside into nature across the whole community and she led by example being the first person at any event and the last to leave.

She got involved in clearing up the neglected site from removing dog mess to potentially dangerous items. Alongside this was facilitating outdoor play for local children by establishing a mud kitchen, swings and climbing features within a wooded area and gardens in the meadow. Standing firm against negative attitudes was her major leadership role as every challenge from paedophiles to hazards from being outdoors were suggested by local media. Using the principles and policies from Scotland's Curriculum for Excellence, Glasgow City Council's report 'Outside Now' and the Scottish Forestry Commission's strategy 'Woods for Learning' Emily was able to enlist wider support from the leadership of local schools. The children loved what was on offer on visits through the play and learning within a place with a philosophy common to forest school practice. Engaging disaffected and vulnerable young people came from providing opportunities to learn bush craft, gardening, and similar skills from mending bikes to parkour.

The Children's Meadow project has encouraged broader leadership and galvanised responsibility from everyone, often by asking folk to lead activities that they weren't likely to volunteer for. This had a domino effect and brought in more people bringing further skills. Having an anti-perfection ethos also helped as it meant people would have a go, or if someone forgot something, another person would step in. Following the ideal that helping community members to achieve what they wanted to do added further motivation and led to the creation of a labyrinth and a 'beedookit' (a large structure to house bees like a pigeon house) in the meadow. This showed the decision-makers the huge potential and value of North Kelvin Meadow and Children's Wood. Setbacks, vandalism, negativity, red tape and pessimism still arise but this community now acts like they own the site and has it endorsed by children's author Julia Donaldson and other celebrities.

'Pop-up' adventure play areas

This relatively new approach appears to have started as holiday provision for children from 4 onwards to get them outdoors more. The concept probably emerged from the adventure playgrounds that Lady Hurtwood established in inner city areas in the 1950s and 60s. They have spread across the English-speaking world and may also have benefitted from the move to include open-ended resources (loose parts) into playground provision, particularly in environments which are flat, tarmac spaces which lack variety and flexibility.

The amazing part of these events is how they appear outside as almost magical, in that they arrive, 'POP' and a few hours later vanish. What the outsider does not see are the months of planning, legal hurdle jumping, sourcing of loose parts, community creation, site and staff arrangement and ongoing social media presence often run by an army of volunteers whilst hoping for kind weather.

'The natural world provides a wonderful circus tent for children's play' (Lester & Maudslesy, 2007, p. 14). The children arrive fascinated and curious, a few hesitant whilst others rush in and start to explore what is on offer. The message for children is 'play and have fun.' The message for adults lies in 'allow the children the freedom to explore the materials, use them as they wish in any area of the play site that they wish.

Outdoor environments are unique as in what they offer to engage young children. For example, some will become energised and very enthusiastic, whilst others will be quieter and more observant gaining different information. 'Studies of different outside play spaces found that a mixture of manufactured materials and natural materials made children more active' (Blanchet-Cohen & Elliot, 2011, p. 759).

CASE STUDY: LEEDS ADVENTURE PLAY PROJECT

This pilot outdoor summer play scheme for primary aged children was run by a small Community Interest Company in Leeds called Lemon Balm. After establishing all the essential safeguarding policies and public liability insurance it offered 30 free spaces for 4-to-12-year-olds primarily to families in 3 council estates in Leeds surrounding the Meanwood Community Centre. The Centre owns a small but decent sized patch of land immediately adjacent to it and the play scheme ran there, with provision of loose parts, art supplies and outdoor cooking/eating supplies stored in a shed within the Community Centre's fenced property. Every session the children were invited to help prepare, chop veggies and herbs, and cook healthy meals on a campfire stove. The leader has a clear ethos behind the provision: 'Understanding children's need for time, space and freedom in their lives as a basic right as well as a necessary step for their physical, emotional, social, cognitive and personal development.'

From the beginning the play scheme was completely outdoors, no matter the weather as well as giving time for children's self-directed play. The leader commented 'I honestly don't think many parents knew or care what we were talking about in the leaflets but by the end I think we sold them on it very well!' Although the outdoor area was not ideal, he also said: 'Not even the best indoor environment can match the variety and possibility of plain grass lot (and a few trees) in a working-class area of Leeds.'

The project was positively received and the leader has further plans:

> While my goal was to make it as full of as much self-directed play as possible, I think the majority of the children were initially entirely inexperienced with such a setting that had relatively so few rules and no adults ready to shout or punish. Adding to the mix many of the children dealing with trauma, abuse, neglect, or the general stress of poverty there were many times I believe we became a 'safe place' for children to unload emotions they have not been allowed to in other parts of their life. It was challenging at times and a learning experience for us adults but I think we are onto something important and unique. If we grow this play scheme, which I hope to do, I hope to give at least a 3 day training/induction into playwork, play's role in human development, and 'Unconditional Positive Regard' when working with children growing up with trauma, abuse, neglect or the general stress of poverty.

Working in areas at an earlier stage of development

Outdoors is the natural place for many children around the world to play whether at home or at school. This, of course, used to be the norm in Britain, children were expected and trusted to play outdoors locally with friends. The community kept an eye and would intervene by telling the child/children off if their activities were annoying, illegal or dangerous. Parents would then chastise the child/children for this and either ground them to their home or distribute a similar punishment. I certainly experienced a great deal of freedom to roam, freedom to explore and experience outdoors in a manner that is rare these days. Some children would only be indoors when the weather was really appalling. Today most children in Britain are not allowed to go far alone. The radius of roaming activity by 8-year olds has reduced from 6 miles in the 1920s to 700 yards in 2007. This decline is almost 90% and sadly increasing. Gaster, S. (1991).

In some other cultures and countries due to economic challenges, different expectations and stresses, children are outdoors for most of their lives as street children, travellers, refugees, asylum seekers etc. I remember observing with horrified fascination as 2 under-fives picked over the rubbish tip in their street in Tirana, Albania. They were looking for drink containers with straws. On finding a number they would climb back down to the street and have a wonderful time blowing air into the container using their mouths, and then jumping on the swollen containers with resulting bang if their technique was successful. Their joy was palpable!

Whilst working on Voluntary Service Overseas in Papua New Guinea I don't ever remember seeing toys in the formal sense of most societies today. The children used whatever was to hand – sticks, stones, rags or plaited leaves to create a ball or a rubber bike tyre or a bendy stick wound into a hoop to run along with. I have since witnessed similar creativity across the Caribbean, Asia and Africa.

The material and cultural aims of toys are beyond the remit of this book however, it is interesting to consider the similarity of outdoor games that are played by children across the world regardless of circumstances. These may have different names but can be grouped into the following categories:

- Chasing/tag games.
- Hiding games.
- Games with equipment such as balls.
- Jumping and climbing games.
- Memory games.
- Hand games.
- Games linked to songs and rhymes.

Many of these outdoor games are passed on by word of mouth across generations. Many include the following skills or skill combinations, all of which of course benefit children's development and learning:

- Physical skill and dexterity.
- Strategy.
- Chance.
- Pattern repetition.
- Creativity.
- Coping with challenge e.g. height.

Conclusion

The evidence from around the world is that a few hours spent outdoors every week engages children, supports development and improves their wellbeing and increases teachers'/practitioners' job satisfaction. The leadership styles may vary but the passion and commitment of the leaders is highly influential in driving forward children's opportunities to be outdoors. Where the leadership and ethos are shared and cascaded through the team the benefits increase regardless of circumstances. Whatever the strategy is called, outdoors is very powerful as a source of health and education as long as it is well led. The feeling of not even realising you are learning outdoors is immensely powerful and leads everyone on a journey of adventures. It gets away from the indoor controls and demands of classrooms that are often rigidly established within education systems.

There is a diversity of genders and nationalities who are leading outdoor opportunities but this needs to be further enhanced in Britain. At the heart of quality outdoor provision is a leader with a strong belief in the power and importance of nature pedagogy and its benefits to children. In the developed world the move to regain nature and outdoor opportunities for young children is again increasingly led by a group of highly motivated and visionary leaders who are sometimes dealing with unusual challenges. Their drive, motivation and hard work is what is bringing back rich opportunities which would otherwise have been lost.

4 Babies and the under-3s

Introduction

There is great concern at present about children not spending enough time outdoors. However, despite the increasing research available, there is very little that looks specifically at children under 3 outdoors. I was told that as a baby I often slept outside in my pram. I was also allowed to explore freely and get dirty as a toddler outdoors. I now see our grandchildren similarly playing in nature too. Parenthood, being an early childhood teacher and more recently a grandparent has taught me so much about raising babies and young children and what really matters: relaxing, giving them time and space to safely explore, discover and learn for themselves whilst being with them as that safe person when things are too challenging. In this chapter I look at how babies and toddlers develop and learn outdoors and how they can best be supported by adults and leaders. The particular needs of toddlers in terms of their development and learning are considered along with the environments that should be established to best serve them. Finally, the barriers and quality factors for this age group are also discussed and underpinned by 2 case studies.

How under-threes develop

We know that babies are born with all the brain cells they will need in their lifetime (100 billion) but babies process information 16 times slower than the adult brain. Their brains double in weight and size in their first year. By the time they are 2 their brains are making a million connections every second. In the first 3 years the brain is growing more rapidly than it will ever do again. 'Resting periods' when the brain is less engaged are as important as being involved in external tasks. To keep these brains nurtured and buzzing we need to provide the richest possible experiences so that the brain becomes integrated and all its parts work effectively together.

Curiosity and fascination start from birth onwards. Nature provides huge riches and surprises as children explore and discover things for themselves. This has been recognised by many including McMillan (1919, p. 2) and Helen Tovey (2007).

 DOI: 10.4324/9780429436505-5

As adults we often forget and trivialise the first time a young child sees a dandelion clock or an ant rushing along but it is a huge and momentous experience for them. The famous environmentalist Carson (1956) quoted by Bilton, Bento, and Dias (2017) recognises these first years as critical in awakening children's emotions– 'a sense of the beautiful, the excitement of the new and the unknown, a feeling of sympathy, pity, admiration and love.'

The sensorial and motor learning in this stage of development is about what Wells (1987) aptly describes as 'meaning makers' as children are striving to make sense of the world around them in so many different ways. This is particularly important when the world around them is very instant and fast moving.

How babies learn

Babies and toddlers learn holistically using their whole bodies from birth onwards. Their senses encourage and drive their physical responses: from holding your head up, pushing down with your arms, reaching out and eventually to pulling yourself up to crawl, stand and walk.

These early senses develop in the womb and continue to supply endless information. Over time this builds up to inform and enhance each child's understanding of the world.

Figure 4.1 Babies learning about nature.

Touch

From about 8 weeks of gestation touch receptors start to develop. Our skin is a receptor of multiple stimuli and some areas are particularly sensitive such as fingertips giving us warning signals when something is too hot or sharp so we move our hand away immediately. This is followed by the other senses and by the time they are born most babies also have taste, smell, hearing and are very sensitive to touch.

Sight

Once sight is established babies will start to focus and then reach out for things held up to them. From birth they will experience positive touch which is about love and wellbeing that provides security. Although their sight is very blurry for a few weeks we can sometimes experience the 'golden hour' a few hours after birth when babies show intense 'wakeful attention.' At this stage they can focus intensely on faces and copy facial movements such as sticking out their tongue. It will take several weeks for them to distinguish colours and then shapes but once those are settled, the baby's eyes are a crucial tool for learning. As their coordination improves they will be able to pick up and grab items that interest them too.

Hearing

Hearing is fully developed in newborn babies. Often whilst still in the womb a baby will kick or jump in response to a loud or unpredictable noise. This startle response continues after birth. However, they do stop moving and appear to listen to conversational sounds at times. Newborn babies seem to prefer the higher pitches of a female voice to the lower sounds of male voices. They become familiar with certain sounds and can tune out after hearing them several times.

Sound is an important area for fascination and exploration for the very youngest children as they start to see and interpret adult reactions to the different sounds they make. We all need to reflect on the sound environment that children grow up in. They are now often subject to waves of sound from a variety of technology and environmental factors. As they are moved around by family and carers these may increase or decrease but are far from the child's control. This cacophony must be challenging for babies and we need to balance sound with silence and serenity too. Sound is a part of all children's lives (including those who cannot hear but experience vibrations and witness facial movements) and is how they develop language. A constant background of noise and music will not be beneficial to language development. Going outside will provide a different soundscape. Sound travels differently outdoors due to changes in wind direction and air pressure. Babies under the age of 6 months perceive sound differently so they hear birdsong more effectively than adults for example. Sound also varies outdoors from very loud – thunder — or very quiet – running water for example. As the baby develops it learns over time to make sense of these sounds and possible responses to them.

Smell

From 10 weeks of gestational age a baby's smell receptors develop in the womb. From smelling, swallowing and tasting amniotic fluid the baby learns about taste from what its mother is eating. Smell is strongly linked to memory and some children will display a very strong reaction to certain smells such as chemicals as a direct result. Again, this is an important survival mechanism.

Taste

Finally, we should also consider taste, as from the earliest age taste tells us what we can or cannot eat. As taste is linked strongly to smell, these 2 senses often develop together. The sense of taste is from chemical recognition of food molecules which generate signals sent to the brain. Taste buds develop very early in the womb and we are blessed with 2,000–8,000 of them. Our tastes change as we age and young children need upward of 30 tastes before they can like a new foodstuff.

Why under threes need the outdoors

For the very youngest children, the outdoors is fascinating and hugely beneficial for their development and learning once they are familiar with it.

Motor development

This starts with babies refining their focus looking at people and objects, then grasping, holding and placing objects. As mobility increases, they learn to roll and sit up, crawl, stand up and eventually walk. Learning to do these skills on uneven ground outdoors makes for greater challenge.

Communication and language

The outdoor environment can provide a rich and different vocabulary if attentive adults can observe and listen to the child and their interests. Through sensitive interaction they can describe the experiences and opportunities the children are seeing, hearing, feeling, tasting and smelling alongside their movements with lots of positional language. Conversation with a young child can also enhance experiences and opportunities by adding further descriptive details as appropriate. For example: soft moss, prickly pinecone, tweeting sparrow.

Spatial awareness

As the child starts to move around, the use of positional language by adults such as under, next to, behind, over there will add real meaning if used in appropriate times and locations. The child will start to experience, explore and investigate for

Figure 4.2 Creating a baby base outdoors.

themselves what these mean in different contexts and make further sense of the world around them and themselves within it.

Social and emotional

Babies are very egocentric and focussed upon their own needs but slowly as they learn to observe others, their curiosity and fascination leads them to watch and copy what others are doing. They also get vivid and rapid feedback when they make mistakes or take risks by taking a tumble and grazing a knee or being stung by a nettle.

Cognitive

Since human beings first evolved, their survival has required them to use all their senses and concentrate deeply to respond to challenging and unpredictable outdoor

Figure 4.3 Exploring nature around you.

environments. When outdoors this trait still assists young children to learn more rapidly and effectively Grahn, Martensson, Linblad, Nilsson, and Ekmam (1997). Outdoors provides an array for real opportunities, heuristic objects and phenomena to experience, discuss and learn about.

Health and wellbeing

The opportunity to get dirty and be exposed to microbes and germs is important in building a healthy immune system. Time in nature is also calming and provides rich experiential learning that is good for our brains.

Once a baby can crawl, being placed on a picnic rug, on grass or sand, the only option is to move (often at an alarming speed). Children build ideas and concepts through experiences and they perceive connections in their everyday worlds. Opportunities to move freely, to grasp, kick, crawl and run supports far more than physical development. It underpins healthy development, embodiment, promotes sound sleep patterns, better digestion and the understanding of night and day. Being outside also helps to build a sense of agency and belonging and attachment with the natural world whilst also nurturing curiosity and the desire to explore, question, communicate and foster relationships. All the time the brain is making sense of new sights, smells, textures, sounds and sometimes tastes.

Younger babies also need the outdoors to widen their opportunities and experiences from toys indoors. So, exploration of items in tuff trays and treasure baskets can provide them with motivations to reach for, grasp, squeeze and pick different things up and drop them too if they don't like the sensation. Older babies, as they extend their physical abilities and co-ordination skills, can explore larger equipment such as rockers, tunnels, wheeled toys, balls etc. The latter may start as an investigation of the wheels themselves alongside pushing and pulling. Tyres from go-carts as well as bigger vehicles can be provided for exploration and the challenges of strength to lift, balance and roll them will be valuable physically as well as providing a great variety of other learning.

The particular needs of toddlers

Movement is our first language and is present when the baby kicks in the womb. Toddlers are the youngest children who have learned to walk. This is a significant life achievement and one which drives them forward to experience movement in its many forms.

This fundamental drive provides numerous opportunities to experience speed, forces, gravity as well as controlling your body to change direction or go faster or slower on undulating paths with different surfaces and slopes. Movement stimulates the production of the neurotransmitter dopamine which helps us feel energised and alert, leaving the brain in a state of being ready to learn as Kranowitz (2005) describes some children coping with sensory processing disorder. Being outside stimulates another neurotransmitter- serotonin which makes us feel happy and the blue light helps us feel alert and to sleep well. By moving around, knocking things down, experimenting and climbing up and down slopes toddlers are all increasing their vestibular stimulation. At this age children need graduated challenge and continuous access to outdoors. Most of all they need space to move and areas not being dominated by resources such a wheeled-vehicles, balls etc. Life outdoors for toddlers is also a powerful stimulus to develop their thinking skills and encouraging them to share experiences and real challenges and make sense of the consequences.

Babies generally develop strong upper bodies through learning to lift their heads and then sitting and crawling. However, once a child is walking these muscles are often less used so toddlers and 2-year-olds plus need broader opportunities to enhance their whole-body range and usage. They need to hang onto or spin with such as bars, to twist about on such as a trapeze or to balance on low walls and beams.

Encompassing space from high up is also greatly enjoyed so opportunities to climb should also be available.

Jasmine Pasch (2014) beautifully describes the needs of young children at this age as 'boing, whoosh, and roly-poly play':

- 'Boing play': up and down movements such as bouncing, hanging upside down, hopping and skipping, leaping.
- 'Whoosh play': to and fro' movements such as being rocked, swinging, running – starting and stopping, sliding.
- 'Roly-Poly play': rotating movements such as twirling, rolling over or down a hill, dancing, spinning, cartwheels.

She also stresses the need for children to experience carrying and moving heavier and less regular objects; pushing and pulling in order to develop their strength, dexterity, agility, suppleness and flexibility.

Physicality

This is learning about physicality rather than physical development. It emerges through 'bodyfulness' which is akin to 'mindfulness' in that young children need opportunities to pay attention and become consciously aware of their body movements and the spaces that their bodies and extremities occupy.

Proprioceptive stimulation is gained through young children running around and falling over. This is where gradients and slopes are essential ingredients for holistic physical development. Many life lessons are also learnt through falling and landing on different surfaces. 'Bodyfulness' learning opportunities develop from placing your body into hidey holes and tunnel/crawl zones, being up high, low down and in a variety of situations involving movement and stillness.

The process of learning about your body 'bodyfullness' starts in young babies learning through cause and effect. It is a pathway to lifelong learning. It's about paying attention to your bodyfulness and its varied movements from the tiny, intimate senses, to larger movements for different activities in different planes, forwards and backwards, up and down etc. It starts in one place and position to feeling your way to discovering new and different positions, then exploring further afield and dealing with frustrations. This can all be provided for young babies and toddlers within a simple grassy securely fenced landscape with a few slopes, hollows, boulders, bushes and trees. Such a landscape offers wonderful sensory stimulation and physical challenge for under threes alongside the choices and opportunities to be independent, to self-regulate as well as space to just BE. This is genuine slow learning which follows the child's lead and chosen pace.

Ecological identity, attachment and the outdoors

Many children have missed out on rich opportunities outdoors to use their senses and control their bodies fully. The levels of addiction, relationship and mental health problems are evidence of a generation who grew up unaware and possibly afraid of their bodies and of the outside. There is a growing body of research over the last 4 decades about the connection between 'sanitised' indoor childhoods with too much time spent on screens etc. and the later effects on their own bodies, addiction, poor mental health, and chronic health conditions in the United States by Perrin, J. M., Bloom, S. R., and Gortmaker, S. L. (2007).

For young children with trauma and other profound issues and those who have experienced far from ideal starts in life, going outdoors may result in initial fears followed with joy and pleasure as they start to thrive. The natural environment doesn't talk back but accepts children who use their whole bodies to experience it. The therapeutic approach that nature provides has led to some great interdisciplinary and interconnected work with adopted, abused and vulnerable children. This has been advocated for a wide range of the most needy in several places around the world (Cooper Marcus & Sachs, 2013; Pryor, Carpenter, & Townsend, 2015).

Trauma can seriously disrupt important aspects of child development that occur before the age of 3 years. These may include bonding with parents, as well as foundational development in the areas of language, mobility, physical and social skills and managing emotions. Providing support to help the family rebuild a safe, secure and nurturing home will help the baby or toddler recover. The work of Elizabeth Henderson at the Camp Hill case study is a positive example. Although not specifically designed for trauma rehabilitation the Bradford 50 Things app aimed at getting families with young children outdoors is a great example of prevention as well as possible healing from an unstable start which is described later in the book.

What does it mean to be <u>with</u> the outdoors?

I heard a talk by Professor Jan White with Common Ground (09/06/2020) where she emphasised ecological identity and attachment. She asked the question: 'What does it mean to be <u>with</u> the outdoors?' She was discussing children's relationship with the earth, with nature etc. The emphasis was that building a connection with nature is about being with nature and thus over time developing an ecological identity. I believe this strong attachment starts from birth and each individual's ecological identity emerges through numerous experiences outdoors. This might be for a young baby in a sling carried by a walking parent for a foggy early morning autumn walk or lying underneath a large tree to experience dappled shade etc. We simply do not know what builds the connection to nature. However, Professor White linked these ideas to the Habitat theory of Jay Appleton (1975). These are the earliest evolutionary experiences of 'Am I safe here?' 'Will I survive?' are evolutionary drives embedded within young children to explore different types of play to stay safe.

These deep play drives are:

- Den building (for refuge).
- Prospect (tree climbing to see danger and map things out).
- Trail (to navigate and travel).
- Source (foraging, collecting etc.).

These drives all have clear links to young children's schemas but are also part of our deep sub-conscious drives within the natural world and are witnessed in our hormones such as the flood of oxytocin when we are calm and safe. Therefore, if you do not have opportunities to attach to nature from a young age your ecological identity may be less well developed and your embodiment less secure. Nature is a foundational experience and it aids attachment and wellbeing. It helps us look after ourselves and is imperative in children's lives. Thus, we need to start babies off by providing them with attachment experiences of nature and outdoor environments.

The particular benefits of nature

The sense of security

Employing your body whilst engaging with nature can provide varied health benefits but also essential feelings of security from being connected to the earth as was recognised by many of the early pioneers such as Froebel, Montessori, the McMillan sisters and Isaacs. Froebel from his own challenging childhood experiences sought to provide children with the solace and nurture of being in nature, Montessori and others like Goldschmied (1910–2009) sought to ameliorate the effects of world wars and poverty in children who were refugees, orphans etc. The McMillans realised that the damaging effects of poverty and poor housing could be improved by providing nurseries with access to clean water, fresh air and healthy food grown by the children. Finally, Isaacs who realised that children's healthy minds and bodies were far more likely to prosper outdoors and through opportunities to lead your own learning via curiosity. This physical connection with our planet can calm negative stress and trauma whilst providing reassurance and security simply by being outdoors in the constancy of ongoing nature, seasons, weather and the cycles of life.

Sensorial gains

The benefits of being outdoors in nature have really accumulated rapidly in recent years and most recently during the pandemic. Most research has focused upon the visual sense of nature experience and its benefits. The resultant physiological changes and mechanisms resulting from sound, smell, taste, touch, and some possible non-sensory pathways have been neglected. Natural sounds and smells underpin experiences of nature for many people, and this may well be rooted in evolutionary psychology. Only recently has petrichor (the smell of rain which stems from microscopic Streptomyces bacteria in the soil that produce a compound called geosmin) been recognised. Tactile experiences of nature, through heuristic play and animal petting, are fundamentally important because of their sensorial opportunities and are often the areas which young children like to explore. Tastes of nature, through growing and consuming natural foods via gardening, have been linked with a range of health and wellbeing benefits. Beyond the 5 senses, evidence is emerging for other non-visual pathways of nature experiences as being effective. These include ingestion or inhalation of phytoncides, negative air ions and microbes in the air and soil which seem likely to deliver benefits from natural experiences outdoors.

Figure 4.4 Using your senses.

Mental health outcomes

From 1985 until 2013, the researchers from the University of Aarhus combed data from *one million* Danish residents. They looked at everything from income to educational level, history of familial mental illness as well as how much green space surrounded where the residents had grown up. As they had so much data to work with, the researchers were able to try and control for socioeconomic factors – children who grow up wealthier probably have more access to green space, for example. Yet even factoring those discrepancies in, researchers found that being raised surrounded by nature as a child meant a 55% lower incidence of developing mental health issues as adults. Even better, it seemed that the more time children spent in nature, the better, as far as mental health outcomes were concerned. This has an important bearing on the provision of parks and open spaces for those living in cities and particularly for the most vulnerable in these areas.

Similarly, a study by Twohig-Bennett and Jones (2018) demonstrated the health benefits that living close to nature and spending time outside have significant and wide-ranging physical and mental health benefits. The report again reveals that exposure to greenspace reduces the risk of type II diabetes, cardiovascular disease, premature death, preterm birth stress, and high blood pressure. This in turn would reduce pressure and demands on the NHS making economic sense particularly during and post pandemic.

A nature premium

Thus, we should be striving to ensure the rights of access to outdoors for babies, children, young people and others in vulnerable categories to reconnect with nature. The concept of the Nature Premium is built on the back of the Sports Premium which provided funding to give children a healthier start via sport and the 2018 government report 'A Green Future: Our 25-year plan to improve the environment.' The Nature Premium is aimed at embedding nature education in diverse settings and schools post lockdown as a part of a green recovery. Led by a small group from the Forest School Association it aims to train staff, embed nature in the curriculum, improve outdoor sites in schools and settings whilst improving access to farm, garden, woodland and other natural sites. It also proposes a GCSE in Natural History and the establishment of a National Nature Service as a resource for all. Ultimately an outdoor classroom for all children.

CASE STUDY: TIME TO BREATHE OUTDOORS

Children today are born with the same sensory systems as babies born hundreds of years ago, yet they face an unprecedented level of sensory bombardment and less opportunity to play and be outdoors. Becoming aware of the additional challenges facing babies born into families with substance misuse issues and living in poverty, I became concerned for their wellbeing and decided to use my experience and love of the outdoors to create a nature-based project for under 3's on Child Protection Orders. I named it Nature Nurture.

As many of the children exhibited anxieties, aggression and depression, my primary aim was to provide them with time and space to explore an outdoor context with all of their senses in an unhurried way, supported by informed, patient adults helping them to discover joy in play and movement.

It was essential, however, that the adults working in the group could support the children as one team, drawing on a shared understanding of the principles behind a holistic approach, centred on the development of head, heart and hands through play in an outdoor context. I therefore devised a training plan to ensure we could work effectively, collaboratively and harmoniously during the project.

Our local woodland provided the children with a variety of sensory opportunities and space to play, so we needed few resources. Each week we took a small cart filled with woodwork tools, mats to sit on, string, rope, a tarpaulin, snack-time food, warm drinks/water, some paper and crayons and small baskets for found treasures.

The children, free to explore the woods in all weathers, were initially hesitant, not knowing what was permissible and what wasn't – how far could they go, what could they touch, was it safe, were there dangerous, wild animals. It took a few sessions to establish routines to help them feel safe and to incorporate songs that signalled time for change in a gentle, non-threatening way.

Within 3 weeks the children showed clear signs of being more at ease in their bodies, and social relationships, rushing up the pathway to the nursery and talking excitedly about what they wanted to do. Each season brought them new adventures and possibilities: snow, muddy puddles, flowers, birdsong, insects, wild winds, fallen pinecones and falling leaves. Over time the children's ability to be present, to play and to be curious flourished, as well as their joy and laughter.

Change brings challenges and in my previous post, supporting EY practitioners' outdoor practices, I noted that practitioners often expressed feelings of isolation and a lack of shared enthusiasm from their colleagues. In response I developed an outdoor Community of Practice within my local authority, called Working in Green Local Spaces (WIGLS), to enable practitioners to find their tribe; other like-minded, enthusiastic outdoor early years practitioners. A Community of Practice helps build a group of local champions who can develop a sustainable future, together, for outdoor work. Training, offered at least once a month, frequently included hospitality visits to other settings to discuss the development of their context, as well as visits to outdoor settings further afield.

Figure 4.5 Getting dirty is part of the experience.

Barriers for under threes outdoors

Given the many benefits, why do such young children not get out more? Perhaps this is because the very young are seen as the most vulnerable? Or the least likely to benefit? Are there a shortage of examples and role-models? Parents learn from family and friends but also what they see happening around them and on social media. Some parents may need to see other babies experiencing and enjoying such outdoor opportunities before they are confident to try for themselves. In our risk-adverse society are we wrapping babies in too much cotton wool? Is there a possible gender bias in that more female figures seem more likely to be involved in child rearing that influences how the very youngest children experience challenges outdoors or not? Or perhaps society encultures families not to give such young children real access to outdoors and all its variety?

Leading the very youngest children

The very youngest in our society are not always seen as worthy of the quality leadership provided for older children. The qualifications, status, salaries and rewards for those who work with this age group are often at the very lowest point. This does not encourage brave experimentation but rather a culture of stress and fear of litigation. If you visit a setting, you will often find the least experienced and qualified staff in the baby room. Babies are not seen as needing leadership but at best love, play and care. This has been substantiated in the Baby Room Project by Goouch and Powell (2013).

If this is what is happening indoors, then what is occurring outdoors? The Froebel Trust funded Nicola Kemp and Jo Josephidou to research 'Where are the Babies? Engaging Under Two's with the Outdoors.' This study focused on babies and under twos and reported back on their first stage in February 2020. This research concluded that babies being in outdoor environments are scarce. There were 2 dominant ideas revealed: being safe and being active. The impact of both of these is to exclude babies from outdoors. Importantly they suggest that different ways of talking about babies outdoors need to be developed whilst recognising the powerful impact of sensory stimulation, sleeping and movement for such young children outdoors. They state that 'Knowledgeable adults (both practitioners and parents) are needed to support these experiences and to develop and extend the environment being offered.' (2020, p. 11) This to me hints at the important role leadership can play.

Main concerns

When I asked on social media what are the main issues about taking babies and under 2s outdoors these were the main responses:

- Settings need a policy about 'a safe space outdoors for babies which the baby room staff are both trained for and expected to use.'
- There can be 'real anxiety about taking babies outdoors.' The 'fears are mainly about babies who are mobile but not yet walking that their might hurt themselves crawling, rolling, shuffling, walking holding on. Or that they might pick up and eat something plus getting dirty hands and knees.'
- The 'confidence of the adults leading settings and the ethos are crucial in giving staff confidence to take babies outdoors.'
- Leadership of babies going outdoors works when 'the leaders are prepared to talk about possibilities, concerns and reflect about experiences.'

Providing quality environments

A setting's ethos, understanding of national and local policy, pedagogical practice, role modelling and staff training is essential for effective outdoor provision for the under threes. As is being able to nurture a sense of trust and value in parents and practitioners for outdoors. Although outdoors is often an optimal environment for babies and toddlers, the focus is often on those who can walk whilst forgetting the very youngest. This is probably the area which needs greatest focus by leaders. The joint use of shared space by mobile babies who are walking and older children can be hazardous in mixed age-range settings with, for example, wheeled toy play or football. This is commonly dealt with by the use of vertical grouping arrangements to keep the babies safe (and sadly often indoors) to give them the ideal developmentally appropriate experiences away from the perceived dangers.

Health and safety

To combat this, leaders must understand child development and how this is supported outdoors alongside knowledge of developmentally appropriate care and health and safety for this age group. For the youngest children the greatest concern outdoors is probably picking up, eating and ingesting harmful substances that most concerns parents and carers. We need to be extra vigilant in our risk benefit assessment and checking areas for toxic plants, fungi, dangerous substances e.g. slug pellets, stagnant water, animal faeces etc. However, we can also rely on children's instincts – toxic substances usually taste bad! Teaching children that all plants are food for animals and birds and always asking an adult is a sound strategy. Commonly available substances outdoors such as mud, sand and most things in nature are far safer than many manufactured items found in most family homes.

Confident adults

Very young babies will sense when their parent/carer is at ease or feels threatened or scared and thus become sensitised that certain places and experiences may not therefore be good for them early on. Also, through investigating movements outdoors and also inside involved in play – picking, dropping, placing, stacking etc. babies observe adult reactions and can quickly learn not to enjoy some surfaces or tactile opportunities if they are rejected by their caring adult.

Other possibilities

There is an important and often hidden role grandparents can play in helping to take babies outdoors. They often have the time, experience and security of understanding that outdoors matters for babies. When I asked practitioners for their views on social media about babies I was heartened by responses and photographs from several grandparents, parents and practitioners caring for and working with babies.

Developing the outside area

Some settings may have very limited or restricted spaces outdoors and they may prioritise time for the older children for these. However, they then need to consider providing rich opportunities for risky and heuristic play indoors instead. One Norwegian study showed that the youngest children actually engaged in more risky play indoors. Outdoors and inside need to include more natural and man-made resources to provide wider variation and challenge to support the risk-taking for the youngest children. Kleppe (2018). This could include:

- Objects that are soft and hard, heavy and light, rough and smooth, wet and dry, cool and warm, things that make sounds or blow in the breeze or when shaken or kicked.
- Natural objects, such as leaves, feathers, flowers, herbs, grass, smooth river stones (must be larger than a D-size battery).
- Objects for muscle development, such as things to push and pull, balls, large hollow blocks, and hanging things to reach, grasp or kick.
- Open-ended materials that babies can explore in their own way – by grasping, poking, banging, squeezing and shaking.
- Containers, boxes and baskets to take things out of and put them back in.
- Different surfaces to crawl on, such as grass, wood, pavers, rubber, straw matting.
- Places to crawl over, under and through, such as a low wide bridge, a short tunnel, a plank close to the ground, a low ramp, and places to play 'peek a boo.'
- Sturdy items to pull up on (logs, ledges) with soft ground to fall back onto.
- Sand and/or mud play to experience wet and dry sand on their hands and feet.
- Wind chimes and mirrors.
- Sturdy picture books and other indoor resources preferably made from natural materials or safe repurposed items.
- Water play in a shallow basin or tray, with 2 or 3 small containers that are easy to hold, a spoon or small ladle, a few smooth large flat stones, and objects that float, sink and have holes in them. (Adapted from Australian Quality Standards: Babies and Outdoor Play Information Sheet www.acecqa.gov.au)

All should be supervised closely and babies should be dressed appropriately

An example

Whilst consulting for a small day nursery chain I challenged them to provide some mud for their babies to experience. I was thrilled when a photo was sent to me of babies in splash suits sitting in mud outdoors with muddy hands and feet. This took real courage and sensitive guidance with parents. Perhaps parental fears are an unseen influence on practitioners acting as a hidden control limiting their access outdoors which they so need and deserve?

Figure 4.6 Mud kitchen.

Loose parts

The cosy peaceful corners indoors and out matter too. It is easier to consider outdoor environmental provision under the Characteristics of Effective Learning which were established within the Early Years Foundation Stage (EYFS) (2014). Start with open-ended found materials such as cardboard boxes, cones and corks. These open-ended resources (loose parts) originated from the work of Froebel and later Elinor Goldschmied. Heuristic play comes from the Greek work 'eurisko' which means 'discover' which Goldschmied described as particularly important for two-year olds because the varied materials provide infinite possible combinations for exploration and sensory experience.

In this world outdoors there are endless possibilities and multi-layered complexities. The numerous quantities of open-ended resources (loose parts) found in nature stimulate several senses at once and provide rich tools for learning. From around 18–24 months, toddlers begin to arrange objects, which gradually develops into sorting and classifying activities. By the age of four years, building, making and constructing behaviours emerge. The choice, range, appearance and feel of objects also change outdoors in terms of weather and seasons.

Loose parts by their very nature can be used in a variety of ways:

- Picked, collected, gathered and piled up.
- Transported from place to place.
- Dropped, dumped, destroyed and rolled.
- Mixed, stirred and transformed.
- Experienced by the whole body.

Rough and tumble play

Some experiences outdoors can also lead to rough and tumble play which has been shown to help behaviour control in under threes. A study by Cambridge University education department in conjunction with the LEGO foundation looked at how fathers and mothers played with their children from birth to 3 and whether it impacted upon their development. Academics reviewed data from 78 studies, carried out mainly in Europe or the US between 1977 and 2017, to understand more about how fathers play with their children from birth to three years old. While there were similarities in the way both genders play with their child, it found that fathers tend to engage in more physical play – tickling, chasing games, climbing, hiding and piggy-back rides. This also has a bearing on the gender balance of staffing with the under threes too. Researchers claim this form of play is 'particularly well-suited' for developing skills that help children control their feelings. Children who benefited from 'high-quality playtime' with their fathers were better able to manage their aggression and less likely to display hyperactivity, emotional or behavioural difficulties (Jarvis, P., 2006 Rough and Tumble Play: Lessons in Life. Also: Zosh, Hopkins, Jensen, Liu, Neale, Hirsh-Pasek, Solis, & Whitebread, 2017).

Opportunities for all children throughout the year

Settings need to provide a range of these essential learning opportunities outdoors for toddlers all year round. This is not about separating different ages and stages, but providing a rich outdoor context indoors and out which respects the development needs of all the children. Some provision will need careful reflection and discussion such as the use of wheeled toys and water play. By limiting access and time to use wheeled toys the children are given the space and time to explore other rich opportunities. Some children can become 'stuck' on pushing, pulling and riding on wheeled toys and need adult intervention to widen their choice of activities. This widening of choice should include many vestibular sensory opportunities such as balancing, twisting, spinning, rocking, swinging, rolling, jumping, tipping and other movement tasks. The development of proprioceptive opportunities via pulling, pushing, lifting, digging, stretching, hanging by your arms, throwing and rough and tumble play are also important. These body senses develop, modulate and integrate together to help children to develop a whole-body awareness and assist in getting their bodies to move effectively in all the right ways.

Inevitably through busy play the grassy areas will wear out on popular features such as slopes but these can be re-turfed or reseeded as part of planned maintenance by involving the children in the process. They can also be used as mud slides (or dust baths) in less clement weather if suitable outdoor clothing is available. Artificial turf is often used in such high use areas but it can lead to other problems such as burns and grazes from falls and it can get very hot to walk on in summer.

CASE STUDY: CHILDMINDER IN THE NORTH

Julie is a childminder working within a team of childminders and assistants. Outdoor play is provided both in the garden of her house where the service is based and in a variety of outdoor areas in the community (woodlands, moors etc.) These areas are visited 2–3 times each week and the remainder of the time the children have access to the garden. The setting's strong outdoor ethos is supported by observations and reflections on children's interests. They seek to provide resources which children can access and adapt independently outdoors despite space restrictions. For example: not having wheeled toys out for the older children all day for the health and safety of the youngest non-walkers.

The outdoors ethos of Julie's setting provides more space for children to think bigger, move, build, climb and exercise faster and be louder. Risk-taking is more 'acceptable' outside as there are places to climb, slide, make a mess and make plenty of noise. The children are also really exploring nature too. This gives child a chance to be and observe life.

Babies and under twos

As the garden is on various levels with steps to the house and the patio, the children use these as resources to practice balancing, going up and down and sometimes crawling on bottoms or all fours. Crawling babies also explore going in and out of doorways, exploring boundaries and levels. Julie describes the mud kitchen as being popular with babies who can move, stir and mix soil with water with utensils to create mud. The setting has 2 large rabbits who live in the garden whom the youngest children enjoy watching, feeding and following around.

Twos and threes: These older children love wheeled vehicles and learning how to use and move them. This can include bumper cars, moving around the garden doing circuits and going as fast as possible to crash into the gate for fun. The mud kitchen is popular with schemas such as containing, transporting, rotation and enveloping whilst role-playing meals and cooking often are the focus. These children also love the water butt for filling and transporting water.

Leadership approaches

Julie is a very hands-on modest leader as a childminder. She finds her role particularly rewarding when the children and practitioners are actively involved in exploring and playing together outdoors in areas they have resourced or facilitated together. Her satisfaction and enjoyment of witnessing the adults interacting alongside the children's joy she describes as 'wonderful.' She also believes that being outdoors enhances everyone's wellbeing.

Environment/Weather/Resources:

- She finds managing the outdoor environment very time consuming. This can be assisted by finding suitable storage to keeping areas safe, presentable and organised close to where the children need them. Salt boxes are a great storage resource here.
- The temperature control for younger children (particularly cold hands in winter) was a worry despite lots of layers. They now have a heated shelter.

Staffing

- Julie says she can struggle when staff are reluctant to go outside although this is rare. She is also troubled when they become over-involved in children's play which happens more often outdoors and then they are interfering rather than interacting as Julie Fisher describes.
- Adults are significantly important in outdoor play because if they are confident, competent, curious and playful their mood can positively affect the play and what the children can do. The reverse is also sadly true.
- A lack of confidence in supporting children to take appropriate risks. Whilst not dismissing these fears, too many conservative concerns can limit play and development. Staff have commented that they can feel concerned that they cannot be involved in everything that is going on in the bigger area outside alongside feeling that they cannot always meet children's learning needs despite the children being safe and happy.

Partnership

- Julie and her colleagues aim to understand each child and family really well in order to provide a consistent approach. Parents are fully informed of the ethos and how their child will spend their days. They are given lots of opportunities to discuss any concerns but the ones who are more risk averse are unlikely to choose their service.

- Parents celebrate the chances that children have to sleep outdoors, along with the independence, physical, social and emotional development opportunities.

Conclusion

Clearly babies being outdoors is an important and neglected area of experience and research outdoors. Perhaps after the pandemic and experiencing a slower pace of life some families will reevaluate the opportunities their young children need? Leadership of babies is another area where there is less research but those who are leading the learning and care of babies and under threes are passionate, driven, innovative and truly committed to their role and responsibilities. They recognise there are real challenges but they do not shirk them but rather gather further courage for their next steps in providing the highest quality experiences for our youngest children.

Points of reflection

- What stops parents, carers and practitioners taking the very youngest children outdoors more frequently?
- What impact does confident and knowledgeable leadership have in creating confidence about outdoors for parents, carers and practitioners?
- What should leaders provide for babies outdoors?
- What should leaders provide for toddlers outdoors?
- In restricted spaces, how do leaders meet these needs alongside those of older children?
- Can leaders start small e.g. babies sleeping outside?
- Can leaders create a plan to develop the opportunities for the youngest children to experience nature in a variety of ways even if we do not have outdoor spaces?

5 Focusing on the 3–5-year-old phase

Introduction

As in the previous chapter, there are no hard and fast rules about child development. In their earliest years young children develop rapidly but at different speeds and in unique ways. Whilst we accept that each child is an individual, we understand that there will be similar developmental expectations in some areas alongside unique development and learning for this whole phase.

This chapter focuses on children aged 3–5 and how we can best lead their learning and development outdoors. It considers the role of the environment in providing opportunities for young children's development, play and learning and how this can be resourced effectively to support this age group. It also discusses why young children need outdoors during this phase of development to enhance their learning about language and communication, physicality and their health and wellbeing. There is advice about the particular opportunities throughout the year and the types of experiences and resources which are beneficial.

This chapter will also consider some of the leadership challenges, beliefs and expectations outdoors including some case studies. We need to provide a different range of opportunities outdoors and consider how practitioners can balance leading learning outdoors with meeting the demands society places upon them.

How 3–5-year-olds develop

There is a lengthy period of childhood which demands dependence upon others whilst the brain and body are shaped by the experiences they are provided with. Children learn a vast array of skills, knowledge and understanding at a speed that will never happen again in their lives. These include such varied things as recognising and naming colours, showing affection, and hopping on one foot. These are called developmental milestones. Developmental milestones are things most children can do by a certain age but in their own unique fashion. Children reach milestones in how they play, learn, speak, behave, and move (like crawling, walking or jumping).

DOI: 10.4324/9780429436505-6

However, as children grow and develop, their worlds expand and open them up to new experiences. They gain independence, understanding and confidence as they meet a wider range of children and adults in external settings other than their familiar homes. They are driven to explore, try new things and ask questions about the world around them. Their numerous interactions with family, friends and the settings they visit and spend time in will help shape their personalities as well as the ways they think and move. The evidence from research (Rogoff, 1994; McClure, 2017; Burke & Crocker, 2020) shows that children's natural characteristics make them successful natural learners. This developmental right is something which demands our respect as they cannot be made to go faster.

Development is a unique interaction between what a child is born with (their heredity – nature) and a wide variety of environmental influences – nurture. These result in children having inherited advantages or disadvantages which will be enhanced or made more challenging by how their needs are met in such areas as: love, responsibility and security; how they are cared for physically; the praise and recognition they are given and the experiences they are offered. They make sense of all this through observation, imitation, investigation and exploration. This helps free them up to them learn to 'give it go' and take a few risks, without worrying too much about the consequences. Through this they learn new skills, strategies and concepts which help them to further challenge themselves, understand more and be understood. In this phase children display powerful motivation and determination to grow, develop and learn. They will persist and persevere over and over again in order to succeed. As Ferre Laevers (1993, 2005) suggests it is when children are most involved that deep-level learning takes place. They are developing the skills and strategies that they will need to understand themselves, those around them and the world.

Children in this phase develop across 4 interdependent and reinforcing domains:

i) **Cognitive skills** such as memory, reasoning, problem-solving and thinking which shape later-life outcomes. Paying attention is strongly associated with later-life outcomes/employment.

ii) **Communication and language skills.** These are linked with success in education and throughout life.

iii) **Co-operation, sociability, openness and self-regulation.** These all help children flourish whilst mental wellbeing in early years protects against poor mental health in later life.

iv) **Physical development, health and wellbeing:** At the earliest stages, low birth weight relates to adverse outcomes in later life. The relationship between physical health and development and outcomes persists and links strongly to engagement in education later in life.

These all are important and mutually reinforcing and are more easily supported by going outdoors.

Figure 5.1 Green-fingered children.

Why 3–5-year-olds need the outdoors

Articles 3 and 31 of the UN Rights of the Child state that every child has a right to regular and meaningful connections with the natural world. Learning and playing outdoors with nature locally are critically important if children are to build strong connections and relationships with nature and become guardians of the world. Such exploration enables children to become more curious about nature and their locality via their play as they start to educate themselves. Today there is growing recognition and interest in the value of nature and its very special contribution to children. In the Nordic countries, this is well recognised in the nature kindergartens and nurseries which are now a well-established form of provision. Over the last decade Scotland has seen a huge increase in their introduction too (Änggård, 2009; Lysklett, Emilsen, & Hagen, 2003; Nilsen, 2008) and this has been quickened by the release of the Scottish early childhood document 'Raising the Ambition'

(2019). However, their distinctive features are not always fully understood. The term 'nature kindergarten' is a descriptive label and those who lead and work in them and those who do not each hold different interpretations as to what kinds of experiences children will be offered. However, each will have its own culture and ethos alongside provision of an outdoor pedagogical environment affected and enhanced by landscape, climate and environmental features.

The outdoors offers a range of different learning opportunities wherever it is sited. Primarily it allows all children to be active, noisy and exploratory. It also provides a range of essential experiences for such young children which are:

- **H**ands-on.
- **O**pen-ended.
- **M**eaningful.
- **E**ngaging.
- **S**ensorial.

Outdoors also provides the experiences not available indoors such as the varied weather, the seasons and direct contact with the smells, sounds, textures and sometimes tastes available in the outdoor environment. These experiences in an outdoor environment also help to foster self-worth and independence by:

- Encouraging a willingness to accept the risks inherent in learning.
- Motivating children to engage fully in challenges.
- Significantly increasing the capacity to tolerate and cope with failure by building self-regulation with the support of a sensitive adult who helps the child co-regulate.

How young children aged 3–5 years learn

Whilst everything young children do in this age group cannot be described as learning, each child develops their own means of learning. Children in this age group need to:

- Make sense of the world by touching, sensing and experiencing, and being with living things.
- Make sense of themselves and the world around them as they interact and engage with it.
- Act upon the world by moving, making connections, building relationships and developing purposes.

How children learn is complex but the evidence (DCSF, 2009b; Whitebread, D., Neale, D., and Jensen, H., 2017) supports their need for the following:

- Being active physically and cognitively by engaging in experiences through play and exploration.
- Organising their own learning through schematic, dispositional and other cognitive explorations.
- Language and communication within relationships with engaged interactional partners.
- Playing with what they know and gaining new knowledge, skills and understanding whilst trying out new ways to do things.

This leads them to:

- Engaging and persisting when things are challenging and being resilient when things don't go the way they had planned.
- Building a range of their own ideas and ways to approach and test out situations.
- The means to creatively and critically sort, group and manage different things in a variety of different ways e.g. problem solving, planning, checking, changing strategy etc.

We want children to play an active role as they become competent and confident learners. They need to understand that they have to make sense of things for themselves and can develop deep interests and have some control in the process and in mastering challenges, so, trying things out and the repetition and rehearsing that they choose to go through or not. These are generally known as dispositions, so some children will be more hesitant and some bolder. Some will ask endless questions whilst others will find out via hands-on exploration. These characteristics are unique to every child but will serve them well if they are given the right opportunities to learn alone as well as together. This takes time if they are to really establish true connections and understanding. They will not be easily changed or altered by mere explanation from an adult, so misunderstandings will take time to change and will come through further in-depth experiences gradually.

As we see in the work on schemas by Chris Athey (1990), physical activity allows children to explore information about themselves, their environment and the properties of objects. A schema is defined as 'a pattern of repeatable behaviour into which experiences are assimilated and that are gradually co-ordinated.' Schema also help children find out about how science and mathematical concepts such as: space, movement, gravity, direction, laterality and dominance are inter-connected and link to other learning. So, they may move from large scale movements with balls, den building or climbing to getting to grips with construction, painting, letters and handwriting.

Risk taking through play enhances learning in this phase. An environment which encourages experimentation, exploration, being imaginative and collaboration, as well as starting to take turns will help the child's holistic learning and social and emotional development. Children will gradually build up information via experiences which helps them to sequence the following possible endless thought patterns:

- If I do this what happens?
- If I do this with you (an adult) what happens?
- If I do this with someone else what happens?
- If I do this today what happens?
- If I do this elsewhere what happens?

We cannot make children learn faster but we need to provide very clear, consistent but firm responses when it comes to actions and behaviours we wish to discourage such as 'Stop, put the stone down.' This can be repeated calmly with signs rather than shouting. Ideally by being alongside them we can predict their thinking and distract when things take a turn for the worst.

Noticing

Noticing is very much a 2-way process during this age range. Young children are great observers and copy adult mannerisms, habits and behaviours so we must provide excellent role-models. They can read our body language and respond to what we say. Throw away lines, such as 'I hate wet Tuesdays' can easily give a very negative impression to such a young child. If we walk around clasping our arms around our bodies in cold weather, again they can read the unspoken message that its cold and we are not happy outside. However, the power of noticing can be both beneficial if we give out positive messages as well as potentially worrying if they have inappropriate role-models.

Thus, noticing is an important part of the process of learning and helps in the acquisition of language. It only really occurs when a child is ready for that learning. It is easily supported outdoors as the culture is usually more relaxed and child-led. However, it is not a neutral process but one that is laden with expectations and notions of value. It can deepen relationships between adult and child especially if we slow down our expectations and follow at the child's pace. By focussing on what really matters to a child in the here-and-now, we give them true respect and value. If we record such crucial noticings we are far more likely to understand the whole picture of learning from the child's perspective. In emotional situations such as

Figure 5.2 Making your own risky decisions is important.

tantrums, it is easy to become upset and react harshly. By noticing, we can gain a wider scene and this allows us to be empathetic and see how life looks through a child's eyes. Outdoors provides a natural space and calmness to make such 'noticing' far more likely as both parties feel more relaxed and at ease.

Adults caring for and teaching young children need also be great observers and listeners too. Noticing in teaching is about responding accurately and comprehensively to the interests and needs of children in a developmentally appropriate fashion. This relies on a firm foundation of child development knowledge plus the ability to interpret this information accurately to adapt in the moment to the learner's needs. These observations will lead us to provide the resources and experiences and follow the clues to enable a child to access the next best thing in terms of experiences, opportunities and resources as well as the enhancements which provide breadth and depth to extend interests, challenges, curiosity and motivations. This is not always easy and can take time.

Language and communication

During this phase most children's language and communication development relates to receptive language (the ability to understand words and sounds) and expressive language (the ability to use speech and gestures to communicate). Being in an outdoor environment can stimulate both expressive language and enhance vocabulary and understanding. The child's speech and language become more advanced and sophisticated as they learn to make subtle distinctions between objects and relationships. Their hearing also learns to filter a variety and range of different sounds not accessible indoors. Here again the opportunity to be in nature and experience the hands-on 'wallowing' time in a different, challenging yet more relaxed environment can add real value and rich opportunities. Reading both indoors and out (where feasible) relevant stories and sharing poems, songs and rhymes which link directly to the children's fascinations is important but should start from their interests. Providing very simple non-fiction guides can also support children too if the images are very clear and the text limited and simple.

Figure 5.3 Using a reliable guide to identify plants.

As children start to understand and manage multi-step requests their grammar improves alongside their spoken confidence and personal independence. Being outdoors provides simple yet limitless resources and cross-curricular vocabulary to explore, talk about and discover more about. They often become fascinated by big words and quickly recognise the power of knowing what they mean. Being a 'palaeontologist' or an 'entomologist' were titles I remember children really loving once they realised that the word was strongly linked to their particular interest. They can start to recognise and name a few plants in a patch of grass such as daisy, dandelion, thistle or name birds such as robin, blue tit and pigeon who regularly visit the bird table outside. This will grow their confidence and interest still further.

Children whose first language is not English and those with SEND and who are experiencing delays in language development will also flourish in an outdoor environment with adults who understand they need more time and varied experiences plus rich and sensitive interactions to develop their communication skills. Again, the noticing role is critical here.

Physical development

Young children develop through 3 main phases of physical development usually by the age of seven:

- Initial.
- Elementary.
- Mature.

This is a massive period of change and development but no two children will show the same developmental pathway. Skills in dressing, moving, jumping, hopping, climbing, skipping, throwing and catching, bike riding etc. will all develop and advance but in a unique fashion. Outdoors has such a powerful influence on children's access to really appropriate opportunities physically allowing their eyes, ears, muscles and bones to extend naturally. We know that children need to be physically active and that this can take many forms – running, imaginative play, construction, dancing etc. The vigorous play opportunities when they get out of breath are essential to make their heart and lungs work faster. Activity also assists their mental wellbeing so they get rid of tension, aggression and this helps them focus and concentrate at calmer activities.

There are 3 categories of physical development which children go through. These are:

- Locomotion.
- Balance.
- Manipulation.

Children need opportunities to experience these fundamental skills. For example: They need the large gross-motor muscles movement opportunities of swinging, digging, climbing to build the arm muscles and pivot points, in order to be able to use the small fine-motor movements to draw and write. It is through varied play opportunities outdoors that young children learn to explore and discover things about their own bodies. Opportunities such as manipulating clay rather than dough enhance fine motor development as it is a better work-out for the muscles in the hands. Their confidence in using the repertoire of physical skills they develop will help them further. Areas such as throwing skills help to provide understanding about such things as weight, space, distance, time and direction leading into mathematical and scientific understanding.

Health and wellbeing

Many of the benefits to young children about outdoors have already been described previously. Giving children time, space and choice outdoors provides real reasons to be more active, to use all the senses fully and to explore what your body can do. There are beneficial reductions to weight gain, lowering of blood pressure, enhanced respiration and the effects of 'happy' hormones such as serotonin on mental health, particularly anxiety.

What should the environment for 3–5-year-olds look like?

Spaces outdoors should be environments in which children can explore, engage their curiosity, develop healthy minds and bodies and extend their own personal boundaries. These spaces must be well planned, developmentally appropriate, secure and safe.

There also needs to be consistent and reliable feedback from trusted adults as children will often seek approval for what they are about to do. This 'social referencing' is the start of learning social boundaries and developing empathy. Through new experiences children start to develop problem solving skills and take 'safe' risks. The brain and body are very active during this time, and even when resting the brain is still busy with cognitive processes.

Heuristic play at this age is a central approach to provision. Offering children access to a variety of objects for play without adult intervention offers an infinite range of possible combinations. A thorough risk benefit assessment should be carried out on the objects for possible wear and tear and the essential checks to ensure no sharp corners or very small items. In addition to a basic treasure basket outdoors for younger ones, you can develop themed baskets including:

- Wooden objects.
- Metal objects.

Figure 5.4 Places to gather together.

- Rubber objects.
- Leather objects.
- Fabric objects etc.

Consider baskets with a variety of characteristics to widen their experiences such as:

- Scented items.
- Rough to the touch.
- Soft to the touch.
- Objects with handles.
- Open and close.
- Different colours.
- Matching pairs.
- Transparent objects.

- Mirrors and reflecting objects.
- Objects which make a noise.

Or objects which link to different life experiences:

- Bathroom items.
- Kitchen items.
- Woodland items.
- Containers and utensils.
- Keys and the garage.

In group settings younger children and those with SEND need smaller, more intimate spaces where they can rest, observe or simply snuggle. Space to move around, climb, balance, roll and swing are important too. They need a rich array of sensory experiences such as a mud kitchen, where they can be physically active, move their whole body whilst refining their hand control whilst they talk about their discoveries and plans. Such a 'messy' opportunity will also be a rich source of language and communication to describe, discuss, exclaim whilst sharing new experiences. A deep understanding of the Characteristics of Effective Learning by all staff is therefore crucial in this age group.

Children love to see how they can swing or climb for example. Over time these abilities grow, and they become more confident in extending their own boundaries and taking further but appropriate risks. If the outdoor environment is overly safe, we can create a different kind of danger with particular hazards for them. Children cannot practice risk benefit assessment easily but with the help of a sensitive adult and a teddy to explain things to on a walk about their setting, they can start to put into words the potential benefits and hazards outdoors and this will help them be less timid and more able to take appropriate risks. As they grow older they will be able to apply this learning to a variety of situations.

CASE STUDY

Little Fledglings is a small day nursery in Berkshire for 2–4-year-olds whom I have worked with in terms of outdoor provision. In many ways it typifies the provision available for working parents who want their children to be loved and cared for yet also challenged and given rich opportunities to progress and fulfil their potential. After a revamp of the building (a former library), the team worked hard to improve and audit their outdoor provision within a fenced area outside the building. They operate a free-flow provision, but the outside is nearly always filled with more children than indoors. The team led by Louise have been

> on a journey from almost a blank canvas based on many discussions as to our own experiences outdoors and our observations of children. The children love the outdoor space and prefer to be outdoors. Every parent who has visited the nursery has given positive feedback about the garden. As staff have become involved, have had training and have shared ideas, their sense of ownership and pride in what we are doing has meant that they are taking on more leadership for using, planning and developing the outdoor learning environment. We feel the need to continue to observe, plan and implement change to ensure we meet the needs of the children. There is a cosy shed to provide a communication friendly space with staff specially trained in ECAT where children can relax, feel safe, enjoy a book or simply sit and have a chat. Staff training in maths has given us ideas of how to incorporate maths in the outdoor environment through language, modelling and visual awareness. As children get older we must ensure that we keep observing their play and adapt the outdoor area accordingly. The opportunities for learning outdoors are limitless and so throughout the year we want to ensure we provide as many outdoor experiences as possible, this includes our garden area, in the community and in the local park We have created an area with lots of open-ended resources, for example: logs, tyres of different sizes and drain pipes. The children have enjoyed and benefitted from spending lots of time exploring their possibilities and developing their games and explorations.

The author has witnessed the ongoing development of Little Fledglings and has seen groups of children enjoying the local park to plant bulbs, going on adventures and making links with the community. Whilst they may not have all the features of an ideal environment outdoors, by using the local park, they add real value and huge natural opportunity to their children's learning and development.

A different case study: Stramash

Stramash is a social enterprise company providing outdoor nursery provision in Oban, Elgin, Tornagrain and Fort William, Scotland. The Fort William setting operates from a field which backs onto local forestry commission woodland. They care a whole lot about the power of nature and place-based learning. At the time I spoke with Alastair who was a Stramash Team Leader but is currently a lecturer with UHI in Childhood Practice and Forest Kindergarten:

> We also know how supportive and meaningful relationships and interactions, with caring people in enriching environments, help humans (big and small) to flourish. Alastair stressed that: 'The outdoors' is **where** we 'do what we do,' but it's our ethos, values and people that really deliver the magic of **what** we do.

They have an outdoor access code agreement to use the woodland. Outdoor play is a central belief and provision. Play is, as much as possible, child-led. Practitioners are observers and supporters as well as modellers. 'Our 'planned' input to play increases when the weather conditions decrease, then our focus is on keeping the children happy, warm and dry. So, there is a seasonal flow to our play.'

They have a mixed age group of 2–5-years-olds which they feel works perfectly. Older children take responsibility in helping younger children and younger children want to 'catch up' with their peers. The team celebrate the following as part of the whole experience:

- Freedom.
- Resilience.
- Wonder/awe.

Whilst accepting and dealing with such ongoing issues:

- Perception – that learning isn't happening, we're messing around, children are feral or won't be 'school ready.'
- Precipitation – Scotland is not Norway – it can be very wet and cold rather than snowy
- Proving it's the way forward – the approach doesn't fit into the established ways of recording/monitoring etc. Local Authority expectations don't fit with our approach either.

The collective vision of the staff team, the children and families, the natural environment or place that they find ourselves, the weather and season all inform the provision and curriculum outdoors is central to everyday provision outdoors.

> I think that learning can happen without the adult input that we've come to expect when we talk about children and young people 'learning.' So, that teaching is something that happens between staff and children and it's also the place that is teacher. Learning can be fun as well as pretty random. You won't find observations based on topics that last for weeks – so, the idea of a 'floor book' doesn't work for our children – they're interested in something then something else comes along – learning is, perhaps, more natural. Auditing will tell you that we're still learning ourselves. We've only just implemented a woodwork area after months of talking about it and planning. Learning at our setting is all about experimenting – what works for children and staff.

Both case studies emphasise that there is no ideal environment for young children outdoors whether urban or rural regardless of a strong ethos of outdoor provision. These two are almost polar opposites in scale and environments but both give children a real, genuine and developmentally accessible experience outdoors. There is no one way! In both cases, leaders accept that the weather is an ongoing factor to be considered and provided for. Staff training and visits are valued and provided in both settings as a means of extending team skills, confidence and understanding. There is also a strong recognition that change takes time and environments, like adults, children are unique so one size fits few. Both leaders have shared with me that despite having a strong vision, leadership has to change as it blends from the early days of excitement mixed with apprehension and stress, through the 'hands-on' modelling and taking staff and parents with you by being honest, open yet reassuring too.

The ideal environment should include the following:

- Ease of access to toilets and changing facilities.
- Easy access storage.
- A range of different sized outdoor gear and footwear.
- Enclosure to keep the area secure and safe pedestrian access.
- A grassy area.
- A good supply of natural materials – leaves, stones, sticks etc.
- Resource collections for different weather conditions, water play, mini-beasts, role-play, wheeled vehicles.
- Shade and shelter from rain, sun.
- Zoning of areas e.g. mud kitchen, sand pit, grassy slope, quiet area/den/wheeled vehicles.

Figure 5.5 Suitable storage for the outside areas.

Things to avoid:

- A pond unless covered by a grid.
- Concealed parts to the site and unsecure boundaries, access/exit points.
- Ant hills and similar natural hazards.

Opportunities through the year

As a child grows, their brain and body not only develop in terms of content and height but demonstrate considerable variability as the different systems establish themselves. Just think about the complexity of learning to walk for example. Thus, we must consider how appropriate the opportunities and experiences for each child. Reflecting on the season and weather as to what we provide are for all the children's phases of development and growth also matters.

Equally important is the reflection of the diversity of their cultures, languages and life circumstances. We must learn with every new child and family and not become complacent. Becoming a source of reliable, knowledgeable and sensitive advice for families who we collaborate with. Asking about what they do with their child and what they have noticed in terms of development, growth and learning is a critical starting point in partnership.

Consider the following in terms of outdoor provision possibilities at certain times throughout the year:

- Balls, hoops, quoits, bean bags, skittles.
- Chalk trails.
- Crates, planks, ladders, tyres for obstacle courses.
- Buckets, pipes, gutters and water play resources.
- Pine cones, feathers, short sticks, stones, shells etc.
- Simple games such as Follow the Leader, What's the time Mr Wolf, Simon Says, Hide and Seek, Can you find me a. . . ?
- Leaf crowns, leaf rainbows, leaf kebabs, leaf prints and rubbings.
- Mud and water giant painting with large decorating brushes and rollers.
- Weaving on a fence or frame.
- Making nests, dens and tents.

The outdoor environment adds further possibilities as vegetation can provide potential shelter for dens, climbing and hiding; flatter spaces and hills provide space to run, roll and tumble and varied topology and rough surfaces ensure challenges to motor activity and can give challenge and a different reality. The addition of open-ended resources such as large cardboard boxes, tarpaulins etc. can enhance imaginative play and the development of complex narratives. However, children need the right of free-flow play outdoors for longish periods of time if these opportunities are to be maximised and prosper as they are clearly going to be limited and restricted due to lack of space and noise indoors. Playing and learning outdoors in these years must be based upon opportunities and freedom for children to:

- Initiate their own activities with chance to revisit and repeat over time.
- Seek and rise to challenges.
- Be given real choices about where, with whom, with what and how they will play.
- Take on new experiences and risks learning by trial and error.
- Develop a 'can do' attitude.

Two case studies from opposite ends of the British Isles illustrate the opportunities and challenges outdoors. Both settings are honest and very reflective about their pedagogical practice outdoors and the challenges they face.

Conclusion

Children in the age phase of 3–5 years need as many outdoor play and learning opportunities as possible. Ideally these should be every day and in an environment with elements of nature if at all possible. They thrive on different challenges and experiences which stem from their own interests They need adults who understand and can sensitively nurture their developmental needs by starting from each unique child. Their leaders need to exemplify a very sound understanding of child development and pedagogical learning in order to ensure that the children receive the best possible experiences which are truly relevant to them. Starting with health and wellbeing and careful consideration of what children need physically, socially, cognitively and emotionally is of central importance.

Focusing on the 5–7-year-old phase

Introduction

Although only a few years older most young children of 5–7 years are experiencing a wider range of opportunities and experiences beyond their home environment, this chapter explores their language development, physical development, health and wellbeing alongside beneficial learning experiences and environmental provision. These children are mainly in school with other influences and new adults and children affecting their development and learning and introducing different agendas and ideas. The pressures for leaders and adults working with this phase can come from external factors such as parental expectations, plus political programmes such as children's centres, non-political interventions such as home-visiting vulnerable parents and school-based programmes plus peer group pressures. We explore some of the leadership challenges in working with this age range looking in depth at the Reception Year and how this requires skilled pedagogical understanding, developmentally appropriate provision and advocacy by leaders.

How 5–7-year-olds develop

In an ideal world as children start school, each day should be an adventure and a time of discovery via explorative play, challenge and new experiences. School naturally extends the range of people children interact with. It is during this period that a child begins to learn the skills and develop the knowledge and understanding to become a self-sufficient and resilient person. Each child has their own personality that influences each step of learning and development. Physically, this is also a time of tremendous growth in weight and height. Their muscular strength, coordination, and stamina also increase, although this may make them somewhat clumsy as they are growing so rapidly.

The brain development of children aged from 5–7 years really accelerates as they gain new opportunities at school, home and in the community via hobbies etc. to learn new skills and concepts. As their curiosity increases, they become more interested in

DOI: 10.4324/9780429436505-7

exploring the world and solving problems of their own. Most of this learning takes place effectively through concrete play experiences rather than sitting at a desk.

Typically, they will:

- Expand their vocabulary skills, express interests, thoughts and feelings often in great detail.
- Socialise through the use of language and ask lots of questions.
- Learn to tell and understand the passing of time both on the clock, seasons and in terms of life and death.
- Start to enjoy dramatic play and take on different roles.
- Read and write words, sentences and texts and increase their independence at using these skills.
- Understand numerical and scientific concepts.
- Expand their concentration span.
- Develop an awareness of their own surroundings.
- Enjoy the challenge of a variety of games and puzzles and finding solutions.
- Extend their own personal goals, make plans and describe how things are going.

However, all these long-term traits are profoundly influenced by how they are fostered or hindered in their educational setting and home. This is linked to how they develop self-regulation and how they take charge of their own learning. Future citizens need to have enough 'grit' to make wise and thoughtful choices, to be able to plan ahead, to be confident that they can do things and will stay the course despite what life throws at them. So, their emotional wellbeing and development are also crucial. Children who are loved and respected will feel emotionally safe, relate well to others socially and be willing to explore new ideas and experiences. They will take risks, be self-reflective and able to self-regulate as well as cope with uncertainty and difficulties.

How young children aged 5–7 years learn

This stage of childhood brings many changes in a child's life. Their growing independence from their parents and family as they go to school and other places becomes increasingly important in bringing them into contact with the real world. Friendships too, become more important as does teamwork. They want to be liked and accepted by friends. The expectations of their peer group also start to impact on how they see the world and themselves within it. As their cognitive skills develop they improve their ability to describe experiences and talk about their thoughts and feelings. This also helps them to focus on concern for others and the world around them too.

Noticing

Noticing is an emerging skill in this age group and very powerful. Children can see tiny details and are often confident in making clear statements about what they observe, even those of a more personal nature! This fires up their curiosity and desire to learn more. Children need via repetition, practice and ongoing challenge to achieve mastery. A sensitive adult can assist by being attentive and modelling noticing. Rather than stepping in to 'save' a child in a tricky situation, letting them sort it out for themselves nurtures their self-image, resilience and awareness. This being 'passive from the outside' role can be challenging as an adult (I've found counting to 17 before intervening helps). In another situation, it might involve adding a simple plant/bird/animal identification guide to assist in taking the child's learning or pointing out another resource to take them further in their learning journey.

Consider this respectful and sensitive example from Oakwood School. Staff observed J had been using string 'writing' to record a list of ingredients for a cake:

J: *'It's the ingredients for a cake . . . butter, flour, sugar and mamma puts eggs in and puts it in the oven to cook.'*

OAKWOOD STAFF: *'J is back in today. We had bought the ingredients for her cake. It was an absolute joy to see her reaction! Cake made and ready for decorating. She asked for a picnic outside. Perfect weather for it! (January).'*

Language and communication

Language and communication skills develop at a phenomenal pace in this age phase. Opportunities to hear and use the functions, meanings and structures used appropriately are crucial. Gordon Wells (1986, p. 32) describes this as a 'code to be cracked,' alongside collaborative 'conversational partners' who give 'clear and relevant feedback.' So if we interact sensitively with them using our holistic pedagogical understanding of their thinking skills, actions, interests and language we can link to developmentally appropriate experiences. Starting with the child is a central principle which has the greatest impact upon their language and communication.

Ways to encourage language and communication

The following are ways to nurture and support language and communication for all children but especially those who are more reticent to speak and converse.

- Commenting, modelling and enriching e.g. instead of 'I like that' add in vocabulary 'I like the castle you've made.'
- Use 4 comments to every question to reduce pressure on a child.

- When commenting or questioning, always wait (10–15 seconds) before saying more.
- Be physically face-to-face with a child.
- Take turns in conversation (serve and return).
- Repeat, stories, songs, rhymes and words – you can never do this too much.
- Prioritise talking time in small groups and one-to-one.

Consider also:

- Sensorial and heuristic play opportunities with open-ended resources outdoors are ideal for nurturing language as they can be anything a child wishes and extend their learning and thinking in numerous directions. Natural objects such as loose parts for example add quality to this learning as Prescott, E. (1987) recognises because they can be used in myriad ways.
- Contextually based non-fiction and fiction books, poetry, songs and rhymes can also help children build upon their experiences and acquire further relevant vocabulary. Having simple guides and identification books available outdoors and on walks will help children start to learn to identify, read and name creatures, plants and their features widening their understanding of the world around them.

Physical development

Physical development is central to this age phase. Typically, in the 5–7 age group children will:

- Refine the co-ordination of their gross and fine motor muscles and their hand-eye co-ordination. This will improve their ability to their use of tools to draw, paint and write with greater control and precision as well as play with bats, balls etc.
- Improve their physical skills and mobility like riding a 2-wheeler bike, learning to swim or dancing to the beat and rhythm of music, refining their climbing, running, skipping skills, catching skills etc.

All children do not develop the same physically and there can be a wide variance and we should avoid making comparisons. Whether children in this age group participate in organised sport or prefer to play outdoors in other ways, the most important thing is ensuring that they have the opportunity to be physically active each day. Exercise plays a major role in the development of children this age and they should be encouraged to get plenty of exercise in whatever ways they can as the NHS guidance (October, 2019) stresses. Play is a dynamic interaction with the environment because freedom of movement allows a flexibility across different interests. Within a few hours a child can move from exploring loose parts, to playing a game with rules, to an imaginative role-play and finally to problem-solving as the complexity of play ebbs and flows. The potential for rich play outdoors in terms of innovation, creativity and transformation offers considerable scope due to the indeterminant nature of the environment. It is not richer necessarily than indoor play, but it offers far wider choices and options for the children.

Any children with developmental or motor delay will need far more time, opportunity and support to gain mastery of such skills. Such sensory learning is complex and develops instinctively if children are given adequate self-initiated movement opportunities. Those who have areas still to develop require a lot of time and energy in stimulating sensory environments in order that these senses become automatic. Sally Goddard Blythe (2004, p. 137) describes sitting still as the 'the most advanced level of movement' which is often impossible until you have perfected balance.

Figure 6.1 Confidence and co-ordination provide satisfaction.

Health and wellbeing

Children between the ages of 5–7 years are generally fit and healthy. However, when they first start school their immune system can be challenged by meeting new viruses and bacteria from mixing with a wider peer group. Therefore, the teaching of good hand hygiene after playing outside, caring for animals, before meals and after using the toilet is essential. Some of these practical skills will have been enhanced by the role-modelling of adults teaching Covid awareness but now this is a part of the EYFS Development Matters, so we have another reason to embed these life skills when starting formal schooling.

Being outside is also beneficial in growing positive mindsets and healthy bodies and minds. Happy children who have frequent opportunities to play and learn outside prosper. These underpin the support gained from a variety of hormones which are recognised as being boosted by outdoor experiences:

- **Dopamine.** Also known as the 'feel-good' hormone, is a hormone and neurotransmitter that's an important part of your brain's reward system. It is associated with pleasurable sensations, along with learning, memory, motor system function, and more.
- **Serotonin.** This hormone (and neurotransmitter) helps regulate your mood as well as your sleep, appetite, digestion, learning ability, and memory.
- **Oxytocin.** Oxytocin is essential for strong parent-adult–child bonding. This hormone can also help promote trust, empathy and bonding in relationships, and oxytocin levels generally increase with physical affection like cuddling.
- **Endorphins.** These are your body's natural pain reliever, which your body produces in response to stress or discomfort. Endorphin levels also tend to increase when you engage in reward-producing activities, such as eating or strenuous activity. Sunshine and exercise, laughing with friends, listening to music or creating it, running, dancing and so many more experiences help to boost the endorphin levels. Cookery, stroking pets, good sleep and meditation can also assist in boosting levels and reducing stress.

The environment as a place of learning

Exploration is a crucial mode of learning for this age group. Their skeleton, muscles and soft tissues are changing in ways that will help them refine their fine-motor skills if they have plenty of varied gross-motor opportunities. As Susan Isaacs pointed out: 'Words are at first merely a way of pointing to things, and but empty sounds until children have had a rich contact with the things themselves, and explored them with hand and eye' Isaacs (1954, p. 74). Movement outdoors is central to exploration in physical, cognitive, social and emotional development and learning. It is linked to everything children do, think and feel. Thus, it isn't hard to see why during this phase children who are confined indoors without freedom of movement can become very frustrated and be judged as 'naughty.' We should encourage a movement-led culture indoors and outdoors in schools and settings so that by the age of 7 locomotion, balance and manipulation are comfortably established allowing the older child to sit and concentrate for longer periods of time.

As practitioners we need to establish a movement rich culture by:

- Enjoying, respecting and valuing children's joy of movement and physicality.
- Valuing and celebrating each child's need for risk taking, challenge and adventure.
- Consciously planning to maximise movement and activity throughout each day.
- Being an active role-model yourself.
- Listening, respecting and engaging with children's ideas, theories and interests.

Figure 6.2 The choice of self-chosen adventure, challenge and risk taking.

Young children in this age group are increasingly being separated from the natural world as their access to outdoors is diminishing. In a study in Australia researchers Dowdell, Gray, and Malone (2010) found that natural environments support children's imaginative play and the development of positive relationships. The environment can become a place of learning if teachers support children in developing their relationship with nature. A central aspect of this was for the teachers to view outdoors not as a break from teaching or 'down time' but an opportunity to interact, explore and learn about the life-cycles of plants, animals, the seasons and weather.

This is dependent on:

- Adults seeing the full potential of outdoor learning.
- Children having frequent access to outdoors, its space and elements and seeing themselves as being connected and part of nature.
- Adults supporting, encouraging and providing relevant stimuli and feedback to enrich learning.

CASE STUDY: ST PETER'S R.C. PRIMARY SCHOOL, LEATHERHEAD, SURREY – A CASE STUDY ABOUT LEADERSHIP AND CHANGE: DEPUTY HEADTEACHER: MARIANNE MCDONNELL

St Peter's is a 2-form entry Roman Catholic primary school in Surrey which has become increasingly diverse over recent years. I interviewed the Deputy Headteacher who described the school's early childhood provision as being 'driven by the children.' She went on to say the staff team are:

> Realists who understand that when young children are active, engaged and autonomous they are happy and learn. They have sensible provision which allows free-flow inside and out for long periods with short sharp teaching of the necessities expected of a maintained state primary school.

They moved from a 'topic-led' approach where children were encouraged to come and sit down to write inside to an approach where being outside provides the real reasons and genuine motivation for writing, counting and measuring, for example, when racing cars down a ramp. They now use a more fluid child-led free flow system because they understand that children need quality interactions, sensitive support, communication and staff who can maximise the teachable moments. As a school they wish they had done so sooner as the levels of engagement were transformational and their good level of development went up. Although the development of different cohorts has varied, all children are progressing due to their focus on a personalised learning approach.

Marianne states:

> You cannot import change but rather grow it from within. This takes time, energy, passion, a great deal of talk, organisation and no fancy programmes or expensive fixed features or material stuff. It is far from easy but real fun exemplifying that this is the real work load of early years. Outside is loud, dangerous and exciting.

When I questioned her use of the word dangerous she clarified it saying that they have an approach to risk benefit assessment which encourages children and staff to ask: 'Can we do this?' and 'Why not?' If an experience is deemed too 'dangerous,' they leave it but otherwise go with the flow encouraging ladders, rope swings, large constructions etc. If something is becoming too hazardous, staff will ask the children to stop and then ask why the children think they've been stopped. They have a culture of being sensibly space aware and using common sense to protect each other.

Leaders are very mindful of the staff journey as it was crucial to define to the whole staff team what their definition of outdoor learning is. They moved from deconstructing the model of simply moving inside resources outside on tables to providing an orderly outdoor environment. Outside is where children have real choices to construct their own learning using a variety of resources within a managed environment. This tailoring the curriculum to individual children's interests and needs for example allows children with Autistic Spectrum Disorder to easily move indoors to be in a quieter space when they find things too noisy outdoors.

They have invested in space to make things far easier as premises are crucial. The building has large windows overlooking the outdoor area and there are no particular nooks and crannies where children can hide. This has encouraged the free-flow approach and means that staff free-flow themselves and circulate with the children rather than following rotas. Environmental improvements have taken the form of funding a large canopy which provides both shade and rain protection. This was not fully understood by other staff teaching older children in the school and was perceived as an injustice. This was discussed and addressed as explaining that early years is 'separate to and different from' the older age ranges and needs more money because of its different parameters. This decision was provided in the form of research and evidenced best practice by the Headteacher and Deputy. The real benefit has been that teachers are free to think about the children and their learning enabling them to tailor the curriculum. Their use of Tapestry has helped them reflect on the evidence they have in a smarter more organised and effective fashion. They can identify easily who needs help in particular areas. Parents access these online journals at home and add their contributions, and children have flip books in school which they own.

Marianne described their former mud pit and grassed area as an issue which became a swamp in winter and a dust bath in summer. They tried wood chips for a while but now have replaced the surrounding surface with asphalt. She stressed that every year group is different and recalled one cohort where digging holes and balancing across them was a primary focus in the mud pit. One child in particular relished this opportunity and was a particular mud wallower! Their parents either love or hate the outdoors. The families who have come via their main feeder nursery which has a strong forest school ethos are fine and adapt quickly. Others worry about their children getting ill from being outside in the cold of winter. The school has adapted their uniform to allow tracksuit trousers and has invested in outdoor all-in-one suits.

When what matters most outside and Marianne quickly responded:

> Staff who have a determined passion for outdoors. The leadership must trust them and they must be people who understand early childhood and child development. Our staff need to really understand the children and what good early years pedagogy is so they can implement excellent practice. The 'how' is really important, because it's not about forcing children into moulds but a way of nurturing them into life-long learning and gaining the skills, knowledge and understanding that they will build on throughout the school.

The specific challenge of reception

We want all children to be full of confidence, imagination and social awareness. However, diagnostic and formative assessments in the form of Baseline Assessment in the first few weeks of Reception alongside documents such as Bold Beginnings (2017) (which focused on the Reception curriculum) have strengthened the demands placed upon young children to increasingly academic and often formal experiences indoors rather than a broader experience of play and learning inside and out more suited to their phase of development.

The holistic development of 5-to-7-year-olds is crucial but often in school their ability and freedom to move is restricted. The pressure of the Reception and Year 1 classroom is immense. Wellbeing can also be affected. Just like parents may put on a child's coat, the harassed adult may put on and do up a child's shoes in order to move them quickly along to the next timetabled activity. This shows a lack of respect for the child's own leadership and makes a judgement about their speed of skill use. Children who are still developing their vestibular and proprioceptive senses may also struggle to sit at desks for long periods. This is because they have yet to develop all the senses to move well such as:

- Being balanced and stable when moving.
- Being able to sit still and not move.
- Understanding direction.
- Being able to assess risk and hazard in terms of movement, staying safe and taking your next challenge.
- Having a strong body awareness sense.
- Controlling your body in a variety of ways as it moves.
- Co-ordinating different body parts.
- Manipulating tools and resources.
- Gauging speed and strength accurately.
- Being fluent in repetition and rhythmic movements. (Adapted from Macintyre, 2009).

Macintyre stresses that these competencies depend on a child being able to:

- Pay attention.
- Follow instructions and remember what to do.
- Use feedback in order to improve their next attempt.

Top down pressure is a common experience for staff in Reception classes. Those children who experience enriched childhoods typically demonstrate assessment profiles of 4–6 months ahead of their peers. This in turn promotes enhanced motivation, independence, and self-esteem whilst increasing a sense of failure in those who do not reach the required standard. Children at this age must feel positive about themselves and the efforts they make or they may start to become disheartened and assume that their persistence with greater challenges is simply not worthwhile because they are 'not clever enough.' Many researchers such as Katz (2010) and Caxton (2008, p. 99) have stressed the need to see learning as being lifelong. Therefore, we should continue to see these Reception children as unique learners and we should be introducing a wide range of possibilities and encouraging their agency in <u>all</u> areas of learning with a wide range of self-direction, active experiences, problems and challenges through play and flexible planning. We should avoid for as long as possible the 'schoolification' with increased structure, rules, routines, directions and expectations. Children who are not performing to the outcome expectations at this age have not got anything 'wrong' with them or their skills, knowledge and understanding, they simply are not yet ready to be school children.

Overall, there has been a political 'push down' movement towards prescribed outcomes away from play and play pedagogies and learning for life This adult-led, instructional model is adding to the widening 'gap' for the most vulnerable and causing anxiety for many children. Political focus on this restricted knowledge acquisition for success in competitive tests is the focus of these primary years

Issues surrounding disadvantage are very complex but more formal learning earlier and earlier is not the answer for these young children. A number of reports: The Field Report (2010), The Allen Report (2011), the DERA Department for Education (2010), and the Sutton Trust Report (2014) have all made clear links to improving children's later chances through the effects of varied interventions in their earliest years. Several have stressed the need to upskill the workforce too. Scotland has recently taken the latter seriously by providing a rich array of outdoor training. Overall, if we nurture children's curiosity we help to extend their knowledge, skills and understanding as well as supporting their resilience. They are then far more able to direct their own learning and organise themselves and generally are far more independent.

What does outdoor learning look like for slightly older children? Are there curriculum considerations for those in KS1?

Many older children lack open access to outdoors. Outdoor space is still a non-statutory requirement for Ofsted registration in England, which means that settings do not have to

Figure 6.3 Experiences outdoors provide the foundation of skills, knowledge and understanding for confident children to grow and develop.

provide a garden or play area outside but merely ensure that children go outside on a daily basis.

Incorporating outdoor learning for children beyond Reception age in a meaningful, purposeful way that adults in senior leadership and inspection positions will accept is far harder than in Reception. There will also be staff members who will find the whole idea very threatening to how they have always taught (and in some cases how they themselves were taught). There are a few simple ways which can assist. Focusing on providing features within the outdoor environment which link clearly to the National Curriculum is a good starting point. Outdoor learning can add excitement and interest to the curriculum and particularly for children who may not get out much with their families and have limited first-hand experiences. This might include the following:

i) A stage to perform on and share writing, poetry to an audience. A small decked area and a few crates or wood slices can provide this. The addition of musical instruments and simple dressing up clothes can add further drama and composition learning possibilities whilst still ensuring some open-ended outcomes.

ii) A story den, large tepee, tarpaulin campfire area or tent can also link to the above by providing a pace to read the class book. These can be designed and decorated by the children who use them in both KS1 and 2.

iii) Story trails linked to books which the children choose and design. Simple picture books such as *Going on a Bear Hunt, The Gruffalo*, and *The Very Hungry Caterpillar* are often a good starting point.

iv) Creating and painting story-stones to retell a favourite story.

v) Hopscotch spelling, word searches by finding letters of natural items to create a certain word.

vi) Using the environment to share, celebrate and nourish real reasons for writing stories, songs, poems and factual pieces of information. Trees, structures, fences and walls can display laminated or printed writing and art/craft work can also be displayed in waterproof areas and containers. Starting with a theme such as leaves in autumn or spring flowers can really nourish the creative desire to write.

vii) Creating an archaeological dig site can drive historical interests and the addition of technology with metal detectors can also prove exciting.

viii) Creating a garden and growing vegetables and fruit. This connects across the whole curriculum from measuring out beds and observing plant growth and yields under various conditions, planting distances and ways of growing to cookery, world geography and following recipes.

ix) Starting a museum, nature table or similar. This can have a particular focus e.g. rocks, fossils and stones or be more general such as spring growth. This can lead on to creating your own 'historical' artefacts by 'cave painting,' 'Roman' mosaic drawing, wattle and daub walls etc.

x) Enhancing physical activity through games such as hop scotch, Nine Men's Morris, marbles, hoops, mazes, Olympic games.

xi) Using land art with chalk, heuristic items and loose parts to create world patterns and sculptures e.g. Islamic, Greek, Chinese.

xii) Making maps of local familiar places in the area. This can bring in map reading and compass use too.

xiii) Making volcanoes with vinegar, bicarbonate of soda and food colouring in plastic bottles embedded in sand.

xiv) Tracking the water cycle by measuring the flow from different sized gutters via down pipes.

xv) Using sticks builds upon schematic interests into 3D geometry and constructions.

xvi) Getting to know how long a metre is by using a metre of thick string marked off in 5cms sections to find a metre-long stick as suggested by Juliet Robertson in *Messy Maths* (2017). This includes scavenger hunts, mapping skills, trails, numbers, data handling, measurement, time, pattern, shape and symmetry.

xvii) A cross-curricular approach advocated by Juliet Robertson (Dirty Teaching, 2014) which models, embeds and unpicks maths everywhere outdoors. Also see Appendix One for further more detailed ideas.

Figure 6.4 The best provision outdoors is open ended.

Figure 6.5 The best provision outdoors is open ended.

What should the environment look like in terms of resources and opportunities?

The outdoor environment for this phase ideally should be larger and offer a greater range of opportunities to be active, collaborate, communicate, problem solve and be creative and imaginative. The resources and equipment should be suitable to the children's phases of development taking into consideration special educational needs and disabilities too. There should be opportunities to experience concepts such as higher, deeper, faster, slower etc. The range of resources will also need to reflect the sizes of the children. The loose parts and materials can be more challenging, varied and offer different textural and sensory experiences. The addition of fabric, cardboard and crafting resources can add the option to develop superhero play if the ethos allows it.

Ideally you should try to create an everyday movement rich provision and ethos with physical play experiences for lots of time, every single day so physical development is part of everyday life. Ample space for ground-based play, steps to climb up and down, and heavy items to move around will assist them in becoming competent and confident movers whilst interacting with the environment.

We can assist their movement by:

- Ensuring that physicality and movement are central values and parts of our outdoor provision.
- Seeing routines e.g. tidying up, local walks etc. as a means of extending movement and physicality.
- Providing an uncluttered environment which capitalises on space with care given to how the space is organised in terms of zones and where large fixed equipment such as climbing frames are placed.
- Providing a variety of levels and vertical and horizontal surfaces for creative, dramatic and energetic exploration of walls, fences and surfaces.
- Having a rich array of surfaces with roots and pavement unevenness seen as an opportunity for children to watch where they are moving. In Germany kindergartens see such uneven surfaces as building in life-long learning experience which will assist when they are old and will then be less inclined to fall.
- Providing a selection of wheeled vehicles including bikes (with and without pedals), carts, wheelbarrows, pushchairs and prams.
- Including places for digging and gardening.
- Including things to lift, carry, transport and things to contain and move things in such as buckets, wheelbarrows, utensils, tyres, bags.
- Enjoying and celebrating their growing mastery of physicality.
- Allowing and encouraging repetition to grow competence before moving on to the next challenge.

- Resist stepping in to 'save' a child in a tricky learning situation (unless unsafe), but encourage them to think things through and problem solve.
- Extending opportunities through challenges focusing on children's interests and needs both individually and in smaller groups.
- Discussing with them what they are doing and weaving in relevant vocabulary and phrases.
- Provide rich multi-sensory materials and resources and plenty of time to explore them.
- Consider ways to build confidence such as slopes, steps and stairs, and opportunities to roll, push, pull, dance, and lie down.
- Ensuring there are places and times to be calm, quiet and still to withdraw and regenerate such as a spiritual/quiet garden with seating and calmer surroundings. Or simply lying down under a tree.
- Linking up with the local community and exploring it wherever possible.
- Being active ourselves.

Rough and tumble play – Hargrave school, Islington research case study by Carla Jones and Rachna Joshi

Our context

We took part in a research project with Early Excellence in which we created an action research question for the children in our setting. We were drawn to developing our use of the outdoors but upon closer investigation it became clear there was a particular element of outdoor play that our children were finding challenging. There was a significant group of children who wanted to engage in rough and tumble style play activities but found this difficult to negotiate and manage independently.

When we looked more closely, we found these physical interactions were resulting in social disagreements which the children wanted adult support resolving. We decided to investigate whether explicitly teaching how to engage in rough and tumble play would have a positive impact on our children's ability to manage their feelings and behaviour.

Our research project

We began by identifying 12 children from our Nursery and Reception classes who were finding it difficult managing physical games. We were concerned that not addressing this key area of learning would impact these children's ability to form positive relationships. We also noted that these situations and play scenarios were challenging for children learning English as an additional language or for our less confident verbal communicators.

Our next step was to seek parental consent which we initially felt apprehensive about, but families were very supportive recognising the need for this support.

The children selected were predominantly boys with just one girl. This led us to more closely consider the gendered nature of rough and tumble play and the role media may have on children's own views of play, as well as our own gender views and implicit bias. We had also become aware of the way in which male members of staff would engage in physical play activities with the children, as female educators were keen to model being involved in rough and tumble play too.

We carried out the intervention outside of the classroom and within the school day in 3 10-minute sessions across the week. We considered the best spaces within the school to carry out the sessions, with an existing timetable for PE sessions. We shared the responsibility between 3 class teachers which enabled us to give the children more regular sessions. This also helped to embed this practice across the phase as we had shared accountability for the project.

We communicated regularly, either daily face-to-face after our sessions and by email, detailing what had worked and what needed to be followed up in the next session. This helped us to maintain a shared and consistent approach.

We established clear expectations for the rough and tumble play with all the children, which was 'look, listen, think and talk' and we shared this with the children at the beginning of each session. We introduced a range of activities to the group. These came from Helen Tovey's research (2007) and included:

- Tangling.
- Playing leapfrog.
- Tickling.
- Playing 'row, row your boat.'
- Tug of war.
- Pencil rolls (with arms outstretched above head).
- Chasing each other up the stairs.
- Jam sandwich (when one child lies on the bottom and up to 2 other children slowly pile on top).

The aim of the intervention was to carry out these activities and movements without aggression. We had observed that children encountering this style of play, whether superhero or animal role play were often interpreting physicality as aggression and reacting physically. We wanted to teach the children to stop if anyone expressed unhappiness or pain. If anyone said 'stop' or 'ouch' the activity stopped straight away.

The children were always asked if they wanted to take part before sessions began. This led us to consider consent more widely in our setting and the opportunities we offer children to give their consent.

Impact

The children all developed their social understanding, using facial expressions and language that was taught to them to navigate the physical play. As a result of the intervention, we observed the children playing independently, without aggression or needing adult intervention. The children showed improvement in their assessment for managing their feelings and behaviour as well as their wellbeing and involvement (using the Leuven Scales).

Sharing the results of the intervention with the whole EYFS team, as it progressed and once it had come to an end, was crucial to the success of the project. Empowering all staff to reflect on the behaviour and play of the children in their care was a key development in our early years practice. Without the research question and the spotlight it provided, rough and tumble play could have been quashed in our setting. Instead, the research gave everyone the opportunity to reconsider its role.

Since the original intervention we have incorporated these activities into EYFS PE sessions and actively teach the skills needed for rough and tumble play with all children. We have seen a significant development in children playing physically, managing social interactions without the need for adult intervention. We are also considering how this practice can develop as the children move into KS1 where we are using the term 'Big Body Play.'

We have been really pleased to see how the conversation regarding rough and tumble play has developed so positively in the last 4 years. This was seen most recently in its inclusion of play types in Birth to Five Matters (2021). The response our project has received demonstrates its value as professionals reflect on the space for it in their own settings.

Learning

An important factor in this reconsideration of play and practice in our context was the support of the Senior Leadership Team. Communicating the vision and the possible impact this could have for our children developed interest and support for the project, establishing it as a priority. It is also important to consider how this type of play fits with a setting's vision or behaviour policies and what might need adapting.

A theme that arose during the project was the concept of consent. The Rough and Tumble Play intervention explicitly taught children to notice social cues and respond to 'stop' or 'ow' as an indication to end the play. By teaching children these cues we brought to the forefront the idea of consent as well as democratic practice and began to question where this was or could be applied in our practice. Some established systems such as school council demonstrated democratic practice, however in the day-to-day conversations and routines were possible missed opportunities in which we could involve children. Consideration of baby room changing procedures, lunch time and the way in which provision is set up for children were all opportunities to review practice through the lens of consent and democratic practice.

This project caused us to consider the role of gender in rough and tumble play. Whilst we have found that it can be boys who more commonly engage in rough and tumble play it is more important to focus on the needs of each individual child, rather than focusing on boys versus girls. All children benefit from engaging in exuberant, physical play which can be observed in running and chasing games, superhero play or animal role play.

This work reminded us of the importance of understanding each child and how and when they choose to play in different ways. This took us back to one of the founding principles of the EYFS and the theme of the Unique Child. Being attuned to the needs and interests of children enables us to provide the most relevant support and learning. Our reaction and involvement as educators is crucial to children's exploration of rough and tumble play.

Ultimately, this project led to a reconsideration and development of practice. This reiterated the importance of reflective practice and matching our curriculum to the needs of our children. Sharing this approach, developing a critical lens and adapting our teaching was the greatest learning. As we move through continuous changes in society and the educational landscape, the foundation of this project began with the ability to question why we were doing what we were doing, and matching our teaching to the needs of our children and current cohort. We want to continue to foster this practice within the EYFS team and we hope to share this message to the wider community.

Opportunities for risky and adventurous play

Creative teachers and practitioners inspire creative children. Keeping an open mind and being able to be flexible and incorporate new ideas with this age group are essential skills. Creating a culture of learning from mistakes, building connections and using your imagination to explore new possibilities are dispositions to grow and value in both adults and children. If we open ourselves up to the natural environments, the seasons and weather around us, we can add further value to those available directly to the children we care for.

Risky and adventurous play is essential for this age group, however, the fear of going outdoors because you might get sunburned, you might get stung by a wasp, you might fall and so on are in danger of damaging child development. Some examples of risky play include anything done at heights, at high speeds, with sharp objects or with the risk of getting lost. However, it's all play and exploring your limits, and games like hide-and-seek are just standard games of childhood. Whilst no one wants to see harm come to any child, risky play does include possibilities of getting lost, the possibilities of having what we call 'learning injuries,' through seeing how fast you can go, how high you can go etc.

Figure 6.6 Woodwork.

Ultimately, school grounds are an underused space for learning and development. The natural year provides new surprises which fascinate children. Their ability to observe seasonal change, draw it, discuss it and gradually understand it is a foundational basis for outdoor learning. For example:

- Looking at soil and mud via magnification can lead to explorations about geology, weathering soil types, and gardening.
- Recording the weather can lead to aspects of meteorology, climate change, and measurements of rain, snow etc.
- Examining leaves, fruits and nuts in autumn can lead to fascinations about growth, light, the influence of the sun and moon, structure of plants, seed dispersal.

The use of real items supports the 'hands-on' explorative learning whilst drawing, painting and photographing builds further noticing skills leading to deeper knowledge and understanding. A collection of fiction and non-fiction books about subjects such as gardening, mud, wind, rain, sticks and stones can add deeper contextual value. In this phase taking the outside in as well as vice versa becomes a feature. So, on the more climatically challenging days drawing buds indoors and on the better days going out, observing a variety of buds on trees and photographing them.

Overcoming challenges in leading and managing the environment and staff

Access to outdoors

Access to outdoors is not enough, the environments themselves need careful management in order to be free of hazards. If free access is not available or feasible, adults need to consider if small groups access at different times should be the way forward. The approach outdoors also needs to be well understood with the appropriate attitudes to play, weather, clothing, footwear, investigation and enquiry embraced. Outdoors for adults is <u>not</u> the place to relax with a hot drink, huddle together and chat. We also need to check our own unspoken attitudes about 'bad weather.' By carrying out a simple outdoor audit of possibilities for developments and enhancements to outdoors we can analyse gaps in provision and experiences. In order to teach outside we need to really reflect as to why we need to always stay indoors:

- How can I teach this outside?
- Can I get children to use a nature journal or notebook as a means of recording learning by sketching, notes, photos?
- Can we buy a few clipboards with page protectors?
- What other possibilities for learning, extending and enhancing can occur outside, which are simply not possible indoors?
- How about investing in a digital camera?

Ways to improve access outdoors

In schools we need to start off extending our outdoor practice by starting small and going outside perhaps starting with an Outdoor Classroom day. Then moving onto once a week from this starting point such as a meet and discuss session after a walk. By focusing on the outdoors, things that inspire curiosity, questions, problem-solving, awe and wonder proliferate. Whether natural or the built environment, children will find things that fascinate them. Then we can start to find ways to enhance these interests and embrace the curriculum more flexibly to start from children's genuine interests and motivations.

This can broaden out gradually at a pace that is do-able and reasonably comfortable by giving everyone time to adjust and adapt.

Building confidence through quality training

Outdoor learning and play must be framed by and linked with the curriculum and it should be a part of each day. It should be part of training and on-going CPD too. Leaders drive the success of outdoor play, adventure and outdoor learning regardless of curriculum. Those who believe in it, value it and are champions for it. They can create a code of conduct outdoors which is centred on safety and sustainability whilst widening opportunities and horizons for all.

The staff team can really benefit from getting to understand their own unique characteristics of learning in relation to outdoors. Some teachers are not enthusiastic about the provision of outdoor learning and in some situations access to outdoor learning can be revoked (as a form of punishment). This indicates while outdoor learning may be offered it is not necessarily viewed favourably, may not have equal status with classroom-based curriculum delivery and perhaps in some cases outdoor learning may be regarded as a privilege. Those staff who are anxious and challenged by an outdoor environment are often far more controlling of the children. This can lead to more incidents and accidents, not fewer. Helle Neblong (1999) wisely pointed out that standardised playgrounds can be far more dangerous:

> I am convinced that standardised playgrounds are dangerous, just in another way: When the distance between all the rungs in a climbing net or a ladder is exactly the same, the child has no need to concentrate on where he puts his feet. Standardisation is dangerous because play becomes simplified.

Taking families with you outdoors

Clear communication and expectations to parents are crucial. Whilst the use of positive messages via photos and video clips of their child learning outside can help, real involvement in festivals and events outdoors will help to build confidence, trust and understanding. This helps to establish a connected learning community and helps link people who over the last few generations may have become disconnected from outdoors for a variety of reasons. Many adults appreciate nature and unstructured outdoor environments having experienced them as children but do not engage with it outdoors due to feeling unwelcome for a variety of reasons, e.g. racial prejudice. Research and recent initiatives have shown that for some families the great outdoors is seen as an area only for white, wealthier families and something not for them. Thus, if children do not see familiar adults expressing their positive feelings and emotional intelligence modelled, they may not feel at ease. Once comfortable outside children can go on to learn so much about the outdoors and the gentle ways of gardening, forest school, beach school etc.

Our relationships with children outdoors are central to them trusting us as well as promoting their wellbeing. Whilst they may not be as inhibited as adults they may do unpredictable things such as throwing autumn leaves up into the air or walking through a muddy puddle with their shoes on. Whilst we need to value this spontaneity, parents may not be quite so pleased so we need to discuss such tricky situations to see what might be possible next time. We also may have to advocate for the child and explain their spontaneous play to deflect some of the potential ire. Our outdoor leadership really works when we are prepared to take children outdoors and explain why the experiences are essential alongside valuing and discussing the concerns and practicalities.

Observation is a central skill

To encourage creative and critical thinking outdoors we need to firstly get to know the children and families really well. Then we need to really listen to the children and observe them. Observation can contribute in a major way to providing the next steps for a child's development and learning. It is not about adding to workload but a central core skill for each professional. The skill of noticing is a part of this observation process within a well-organised outdoor environment. It is firmly built upon the environment being designed within and just ahead of their developmental phases. We need to use all of our senses and consider what is actually below the surface of children's actions and behaviours if we are to maximise their meaningful first-hand experiences. Then we can plan the next steps in their journey alongside them.

Noticing is a 2-way activity with powerful implications. I recently met a young father in our local park whom I taught when he was 3. Then he was very unsure of himself and whether he wished to leave his mother and stay in nursery. Having noticed his interest in

Figure 6.7 Trusting the child.

nature I wore a picture badge of a different form of wildlife every day. He soon grasped the idea that coming in was worth it to find out which creature I would be wearing and how we would continue to learn more about it through stories, small role-play and outdoor explorations and walks. He still remembered me and the badges and he became a marine biologist!

Considerations and concerns as an individual teacher

For the individual teacher there are various considerations and constraints which can challenge them:

- Senior leadership, governors or Ofsted who may not understand or approve of my outdoor teaching.
- The children may get hurt.
- The children may not progress, receive the necessary curriculum content and I may not have time to teach all that is required of me.
- I may not have the skills, knowledge and understanding to teach and lead outside.
- I may not have the same authority and end up looking stupid outdoors.
- The children may be more challenging and I may not be able to control them outdoors and intervene appropriately.
- Parents will complain.

Outdoor play and learning does not happen in isolation but rather as a central core aspect to curricular provision. There can also be a tension between going outside and its clear benefits for the children and the vast demands of senior leadership, Ofsted and the government. Perhaps a way forward at this time is through providing a fluid balance of guided teaching and learning outside alongside spontaneous opportunities with interdisciplinary possibilities? This is where thoughtful planning and the ability to shift gears quickly can come into play.

Learning to lead as a child

There is also a vastly overlooked aspect of children's experiences outdoors in terms of their own experiences of becoming leaders. If we put deadlines on learning and structure our teaching and their learning pathways formally and control all that they experience and do in school, then we destroy their opportunities to tread self-chosen routes. Teachers can empower children to take the lead in their learning by encouraging their fascination and curiosity. We give them the 'keys to open doors and windows' but must resist the temptation to shove them through, encouraging them to move through at their own pace.

CASE STUDY: OAKWOOD SCHOOL, LEEDS

An exemplar of using creativity outdoors and in within the curriculum is Oakwood School in Leeds. Look at their aims, hopes and beliefs:

- We offer provision that is rich in possibilities, providing children with exciting environments of enquiry and discovery. We respect children's choices, encouraging them to be curious and creative in their play. It is so rewarding for us to see how the characteristics of effective learning develop as the children thrive and become confident, enthusiastic learners.
- Children have the freedom to explore, question their findings and take time to reflect. We respond to each child, supporting them with relevant skills, resources and experiences. Children have a voice and know that they have been listened to.
- We believe that the whole child is important, valuing their unique interests, abilities and fascinations. Seeing how our children's ideas emerge as the year goes on is so rewarding. No two years are ever the same!
- Our Unit is a community of learners. By learning alongside each other, adults and children can listen to the many forms of expression and communication used. We share ideas and inspire each other every day!
- The work in our Unit is developed through dialogue, negotiation, participation and imagination, while respecting everyone's ideas, cultures and beliefs. We celebrate the culturally diverse nature of our setting, building strong relationships within our community. We feel privileged in our setting to have an opportunity to meet people with roots from all over the world.
- By fostering a love of nature, we hope that our children will develop a strong sense of responsibility, connecting with the world in which they live. It is a joy to see how our children react to the beauty and diversity of the natural world, whether this is through art, dance, talk or play.

Positive messages

The language and phrases we use when alongside children and team members rising to challenges outdoors which involve risk taking should be carefully considered if we wish to foster their positive awareness of the environment and the maximum use of their bodies.

To foster body and environmental awareness we should try to use phrases such as:

- Try moving your feet/hands carefully, quickly, slowly and firmly.
- Do you feel secure on that branch, rock, close to the fire?

- Notice how these branches are strong and thick, or these rocks are wobbly and slippery.
- Are you feeling excited, nervous, hot, cold, tired?

To encourage problem solving we can try:

- What is your plan?
- What can you use to dig that hole, get across the stream?
- Who will be helping you?
- Where can you put your foot, hand, body, rock?

Michael Rosen (2010) discusses the importance of reflecting upon our responses in the foreword to *Born Creative*. He stresses that creativity is often part of the organisational role of the leader. However, the leader should use sensitivity and democracy to make allowances for unique differences and varied communication pathways. Creative learning outdoors involves many different aspects of play – investigation, exploration, discovery, invention, co-operation and collaboration at different phases. The focus should not be on a process of getting things right but using process to discover a variety of different ways and means rather than merely getting things right or wrong. Then we can celebrate achievements too.

Parent partnership

Parents are a much-maligned group in my experience when it comes to outdoors. Since the EPPE project (2004) demonstrated the effect of a strong home learning environment which was tangible even when children were 6 or 7 years old, parents are still often an afterthought in school practice. However, if outdoor provision is to be really valued, their engagement in a partnership involving outdoors can be immensely useful.

Economic issues: Government policy is to encourage parents back into work when children are increasingly younger than they used to be. Most parents have the best interests of their child at heart, although many may not fully understand the significance of their child's development. Parents who are out of work and suffering economically alongside those who are time-poor parents are sadly a common situation today. Many work shifts and travel long distances to and from work but at the end of the day, taking their child outside for a walk or similar may not be high on the 'must do' agenda. The gender of the parent may also affect how at ease they feel in settings and schools which are usually female dominant.

Induction and transition from the foundation stage

With regard to outdoor play and learning, they need to be engaged in order to understand what you are aiming to achieve and what outdoors can do for each child if they are not to see outdoors as a waste of 'learning time.' So, during induction it is important to explain 'what you do and why you do it.' If this is clearly addressed the family will be more comfortable and the child at ease. Staff need to continually provide a variety of PR information which demonstrates what the children are learning and why in order to make it very visible providing a rich picture throughout the year. This can be achieved via the website, newsletters, children's records, short films and photos on the whiteboard in the entrance area all explaining and celebrating the learning being achieved outdoors.

Community issues

Parents today are greatly influenced by what other parents say and by social media. Thus, parents at the 'school gate' overhearing discussions of what a particular child or teacher is doing or not doing can be hugely influential in a positive or less than positive perspective of the class, the school and its leadership. Every parent wants the very best for their child, but parents do not always have reliable information as to what that should be and how it should be presented.

Health and safety concerns

The health and safety aspects of children being outdoors need to be clearly explained by a senior staff member to parents from induction onwards. The details of good leadership, procedural practice, supervision, regular audits, risk benefit assessments and careful consideration of the uniqueness of children at different stages of development will all be relevant. The staff team must be aware that all outdoor surfaces, features, materials, equipment and resources all weather and are subject to heavy wear and tear. Thus, during setting up and tidying up, they need to withdraw damaged or worn items and ensure that the senior leaders are aware of damage and wear. Then budget and planned maintenance can be applied before harm occurs. If you are planning to change or develop your outdoor space, involve parents and the local community as much as possible. Be clear about your aims and ethos and accept their contributions in whatever form they come, even if you may not always use them. Collecting loose parts and open-ended resources are particularly valuable.

Linking the curriculum to the benefits of outdoors

It is also important to carefully explain to parents that children in this age phase are still very young and should not be set too many limits or be prevented from playing for long periods of time outside which could lead to:

- Too much time without movement and physical and emotional frustration, anxiety and anger.
- Children being overweight or obese.

- Limited ability to get on with others.
- Poor physical skills, such as the ability to throw, to run and to balance.
- Reduced self-confidence.
- Reduced ability to concentrate.
- Reduced ability to cope with new and different situations or to solve problems.
- Reduced creativity.

By building connections with families it is essential to understand their goals for their child/children as well as their perceptions of what is a quality education. These can help them to see that mud and mess, the weather and cleanliness are all part of the learning process. Some parents may feel insecure about their child being outside and feel that their choice of school may have been a mistake, so clearer the explanations we can provide of children's progress and success indoors and out will help build confidence that the school doing its utmost for each and every child.

Cultural concerns: With the vast diversity of families accessing early childhood provision we need to really listen to their goals and needs particularly in relation to outdoors. With some families there may be a lack of alignment and they may see their views as marginalised particularly in regard to general play practice. Others may see the status quo being supportive only towards those who have traditionally accessed early childhood education. A good example is being respectful of rules and questioning rules in particular circumstances. Many cultures value structure and conformity, whilst others will be more relaxed in their interpretations. The capacity of the leadership and staff to spend time really getting to know and understand the diversity of values and views is a genuine issue with time poor parents and very busy staff. However, the mismatch of views is important, particularly within formal schooling as the communication can then break down. It also raises important issues as to how staff assert their sound pedagogy outdoors when it conflicts with what families really value. This I suspect is why many schools stick to the tried and tested method of lessons and playtimes.

Other parents may not have been born in Britain or may not be fluent or have limited levels of language which acts as a barrier to their engagement. Some cultures may find the weather and being outdoors actually makes them uncomfortable for a wide variety of reasons. The creation of a welcoming environment is often established indoors but is often neglected outdoors in my experience so this is something to consider in terms of messages and environmental provision. Standing outside waiting in pouring rain or picking up a wet buggy for the journey home are not conducive to a warm communicative handover, however brief. One positive effect of the pandemic in many settings and schools working a bubble system has meant that handovers have happened outdoors as it has been safer. Whilst these have had to happen recently, some professionals have retained the practice and some have even had parents' meetings outdoors too. The support of a sensitive key worker or teacher may be just the catalyst needed here to help parents feel at ease, to discuss the ethos of outdoor play and learning. The transition of settling in a new child is also often easier outdoors where space and freedom are more easily provided. During this important phase it is crucial to discover what the child's experiences have been of outdoors as these will provide some basis to their next steps and the widening of their horizons.

Growing understanding in what children need

Ultimately, partnership with parents is about growing trust through shared understanding. As educators we must remember that parents spend more time with their children and know them best. We, however, see them in a particular environmental context. That's why seeing children outside the classroom and on trips, visits and expeditions is so crucial in widening our understanding of each child's uniqueness. If we only measure their achievements and progress from a Baseline Assessment and further academic tests, can we really say that we know them and their strengths and areas for development? We need to work with parents to build a strong and confident foundation for each and every child. We should remember that not every parent will have experienced the magic, awe and wonder of nature giving us the drive to explore, to discover and develop a much wider skill set than is possible indoors. They may need more detailed explanations and reminders as to why the following are so important under the age of 7:

- Expressing themselves.
- Interacting with others.
- Making choices.
- Testing ideas and materials.
- Creating.
- Developing and practicing skills.
- Stimulating curiosity.
- Developing consideration for others and independence.
- Exploring and making discoveries.
- Solving problems.
- Persevering in the face of difficulties and uncertainties.

Explaining the principles and practice behind outdoors as a classroom denotes it is a space that is, 'a primary environment for children (Nelson)' where anything that can be done inside of a classroom can be accomplished outdoors.

Conclusion

Play and learning outdoors are of central importance during this phase of development. The richer, more varied, yet orderly the environment indoors and out, the more active and imaginative the potential play and learning are, and the more life skills the children have the chance of developing. Going outdoors every day provides opportunities to discover more for themselves about their world. It will offer both fun and challenge, decision-making, innovation, problem-solving, rule following and creation, collaboration and co-operation. Ideally, they should be as 'safe as necessary' because the world is full of hazards. Learning about these potential hazards and the mistakes are life skills. These are also far more likely to be experienced and responded appropriately to within a rich and varied outdoor environment with a rich range of resources, material and equipment. Ultimately, this is about high-quality leadership understanding that we are not simply preparing children for what comes next in their lives but in giving them lifelong learning. We must see children as people with rights, which need to be respected in the here and now with the right to play and learn outdoors, the right to freedom, love, dignity and being valued for who I am and not what I do or don't do. Children need to lead happy and fulfilled lives and be people who will rise to the challenges of the world using resilience, creativity, imagination, compassion, determination and understanding. This they will only fully achieve with our knowledgeable assistance and leadership.

7 The essence of outdoor leadership

Introduction

This chapter focusses on the central aspects of being a leader outdoors. It considers how our beliefs and values influence our leadership outside and the qualities that are central to being an outdoor leader. It reflects upon outdoor leadership in relation to what young children need, what adults need and what should be provided in terms of curriculum. Finally it moves on to discuss what leadership looks like in outdoor environments.

Beliefs and values

We must start by understanding how beliefs and values are central to what we do, provide and achieve outdoors. Our pedagogy, provision and practice are all shaped and embedded in our beliefs and values and, because we are all unique in our life experiences, they vary considerably. Muddy Faces which is led by Liz Edwards in partnership with Professor Jan White have long advocated using your values to create a firm basis outdoors. Values are the basis of beliefs but to turn them into principles and pedagogy takes considerable professional skill, understanding, knowledge, time and experience. This is the foundation of being an outdoor leader.

Here are some key leadership elements affected by beliefs and values:

- Quality educational pedagogy and care provision outdoors that adds value to children's learning outcomes.
- The development of a diverse range of adult skills, knowledge and understanding about outdoors.
- Genuine inclusion and diversity.
- Putting relationships, wellbeing, emotional security, trust, respect, equality and empowerment at the heart of outdoor provision.

DOI: 10.4324/9780429436505-8

Qualities of being an outdoor leader

Various factors influence how we grow, nurture and value great outdoor leaders. There are many examples in the literature and practice on what traits and behaviours a 'good' or 'effective' outdoor leader should display (Martin, Cashel, Wagstaff, & Breunig, 2006; Shooter, Sibthorp, & Paisley, 2009). The most obvious of these are the brick wall model described by Priest and Gass (1997, 2005) who introduced the terms hard, soft, and meta skills. This model of bricks representing skills is of limited value in terms of gender and aspects of bias. Across many disciplines the term 'effective' is difficult to define as it includes aspects of personality, leadership and emotional intelligence. Studies of outdoor adventure education (Ewert & Sibthorp, 2014; Scrutton & Beames, 2015) looked at these three aspects in depth. Many personality features studied linked to transformational and transactional leadership (Avolio & Bass, 2004; Bartone, Eid, Johnson, Laberg, & Snook, 2009). Currently situational leadership seems to be the favoured term particularly in relation to outside leadership but more research to study the impact of cultural and gender variance is required.

Situational leadership

Situational leadership means adapting your style to each unique situation or task to meet the needs of the team or team members. Ken Blanchard and Paul Hersey developed the Situational Leadership theory in 1969. They believe that there is no 'one size fits all' leadership style. The situational theory of leadership suggests that **no single leadership style is best**. Instead, it depends on which type of leadership and strategies are best suited to the task. This then I feel describes the type of outdoor leadership which both encompasses the vagaries of learning and teaching outdoors alongside the social complexity of group dynamics in early childhood where leaders are working closely with a staff team, outside professionals, families and children and often altogether. This vast complexity of interaction requires sophisticated and complex communication skills to enhance relationships and encourage productive social interactions. Team building and conflict resolution outdoors will be essential, alongside understanding the specific expectations of and requirements for working with young children and parents especially outdoors where there are potentially more hazards.

Leadership in early childhood outdoors exercises considerable autonomy in how responsibilities are fulfilled. The quality of pedagogical practice underpins children's experiences outside too, so outdoor leaders need to understand how to meet challenges and opportunities in ways that best suit the needs of the whole group. Thus, they need a range of organisational, management and technical skills and expertise. The degree of professional isolation can also mean that professional judgements must be exercised quickly, confidently and independently. Therefore, being a good learner with sound decision-making and problem solving-skills is essential too.

The characteristics of being an outdoor leader

Thus we come to the crux of what is the essence of being an outdoor leader. Let us consider several important questions:

- *What is the essence of outdoor leadership?*

Effective learning is a central feature of being a quality outdoor leader. Our own unique life experiences and role models outdoors plus our acquired ideologies, ethics, beliefs and values all help to shape our understanding of what children need in terms of the outdoors, education, care and childhood. They also influence how we lead, how we see other outdoor leaders and how we encourage leadership in children. Ultimately, a successful outdoor leader is one that finds the best ways for children they work with in a particular context in collaboration with other involved adults, to benefit from the outdoor environment and to play and learn effectively together within it.

- *Is it about unique adults who are born and not made?*

I believe that both these types of leaders exist. Some educators are lucky enough to have been nurtured and encouraged through their own lives to understand and value the great outdoors. Others will have found their passion and interest later in life possibly through chance experiences, life choices, professional training or through the influence of appropriate role models. This adds future empowerment to the essence of outdoor leadership.

- *Is it about experience, pedagogical training and professionalism?*

How adults experience, learn and gain the professional skills and understanding to become quality outdoor leaders is often down to being part of an outdoor professional learning community (OPLC). The leadership of a PLC is well recognised as complex and an OPLC is more complex still. The OPLC needs to determine the various strategies, processes and procedures which enable the vision to be implemented and the practice to be provided outdoors. Often the main focus traditionally has been on indoors to the neglect of outdoors. Thus to be a truly effective wholesome OPLC, a multi-dimensional approach is required. This is not an individual effort but one in which many are involved, championed and encouraged by the formal leader sharing leadership power, influence and decision-making with a team to benefit children.

- *Is it a blend of all these factors, values, beliefs, influences and experiences?*

Yes, I believe that leadership outside, in order to be effective, has to mix, blend and evolve all of these. A useful way of bringing these important aspects of outdoor leadership together is the application of the Characteristics of Effective Learning. (COEL)

The COEL are statutory elements of the English Early Years Foundation Stage, and so are central to leadership responsibilities for children indoors and outside. By applying its key aspects to adult outdoor leadership, we can also see an effective way of describing, nurturing and supporting the essence of an ideal outdoor leader and their later successional leaders. Through a central focus on COEL and how the context supports and extends these in babies, children and adults, outdoor leaders have a means to develop and improve the quality of their whole provision, whilst relating them to the unique beliefs, values and goals of the setting/school.

The Characteristics of Effective Learning (COEL) for children are as follows:

- Playing and exploring.
- Active learning.
- Creating and thinking critically.

These when applied to leadership outdoors these COEL can be seen as:

- ***Adults who value, respect, understand and role-model playful and exploratory learning.***

  They are able to encompass the views and experiences of others whilst appreciating that learning, creativity and confidence take time to develop. Through the provision of adult carefully targeted reading, collaborating on planned opportunities, going on courses and observing best practice you can build and develop the professional skills, understanding and knowledge of team members before sharing the leadership responsibilities with them. Valuing contributions from colleagues, parents and children helps them to be genuinely included and valued too. Being able to have fun as a part of learning outdoors is also a central feature. Through fun, everyone relaxes and are more able to follow interests and dispositions.

- ***Adults who are physically, emotionally and cognitively active and open to the possibilities and opportunities available to children outdoors and to those experiences initiated by children themselves.***

  This is about the quality of pedagogical confidence and skills and being at ease with the materials, resources, plants, wildlife, and all that entails being outdoors. Knowledge, understanding and skills – with the help of apps and simple guides help you to lead outdoors. Such tools will help you identify and become familiar with the plants, insects, birds and animals you are likely to come across outside. You can also demonstrate being a learner through their use.

- ***Adults who are open-minded, adaptable, flexible and well prepared and include all stakeholders. They will welcome a range of approaches, practices,***

views and ideas from children and other adults within the learning community outdoors.

As an enthusiastic role model your keenness for being outside is evident through all seasons and conditions so you maximise the opportunities that puddles, mud, snow etc. offer. Your attitudes and outlook also convey crucial spoken messages to adults and children as well as those who read your body language. Children follow body language as much as your words.

Being a role model

As the official leader in a setting or school, outdoors can present particular challenges. Ultimately, we need to reflect upon which kinds of education we wish to offer and what benefits children may gain from our vision. This is often described as leading from the front but if used wisely it can be about showing by doing. If colleagues see the formal leader involved in teaching outside in cold, wet weather, getting cold and dirty they will gradually come to understand that this is a team approach, rather than a top down separation. Leaders earn the respect they are given in an OPLC in how they treat others and grow their leadership skills.

Leadership in early childhood is very much about being a role-model for others but it is also about being a model of lifelong learning. This is clearly crucial when we understand that many children and adults never really understand the joy of being outdoors and in nature.

Rodd (2006) lists the following leadership characteristics as being related to lifelong learning and being a learning focussed person:

- Curiosity.
- Honesty.
- Courtesy.
- Courage.
- Compassion.

Claxton (2002) talks of dispositions for lifelong learning:

- Resilience
- Resourcefulness.
- Reflectiveness.
- Reciprocity.

Rodd (2006) recognised how early childhood staff are working in a socio-political context and she celebrated my research (2003) in which I linked leadership to learning because the leader subtly nurtures collaborative learning by acting as a model, learner and facilitator so it links closely with situational leadership. This is not a model of leadership characterised by being in control, being right, and invulnerable but one of shared leadership where confident, trustworthy leaders are respected, valued and supported because they model curiosity, honesty, courage, compassion, resilience, resourcefulness, reflectiveness and reciprocity.

Firstly it is about being consistent in your attitudes and behaviours. You cannot expect staff to buy into your vision if you don't follow the basic principles of that vision yourself. If you want staff to have high expectations for all, inside and **out,** you need to demonstrate the same through what you say, what you do inside **and out,** and in every decision big or small you make. If you want staff to advance their learning, then you have to give them time and resources to do so, while ensuring you advance your own learning, too.

Secondly, it is about modelling these characteristics of good practice every day if at all possible. You earn the respect you are given rather than hiding behind an official title. My chosen title was 'head learner,' and I am aware that one of the most significant ways in which I led and motivated my staff was the fact that I taught most days in a variety of different ways.

In short, good leaders lead by providing an excellent example of learning and leadership. If that example is poor, then eventually the experience of staff and children in that school/setting will also be poor. Being humble and apologising when you make mistakes is as important as celebrating the great achievements, in fact more so!

Sharing leadership and decision-making

This can be very challenging as a process. Ideally it is about developing a collegiate relationship which empowers and enables staff and in turn enables children and families. However, many adults in education and care have really only experienced a traditional management style with the hierarchical leader. So if this appears absent, some adults will question and challenge in order to make sense and meaning of an unfamiliar situation. It takes time to forge and enculture adults into this team contribution model whilst still providing the highest quality education and care. It is characterised by traits such as involvement, openness and trust with a strong sense of belonging and self-regulation. Whalley (2005) describes this as 'power for' rather than 'power over.' These concepts are developed further by Pansardi and Bindi (2021). It requires adults to understand that sharing power provides the real opportunity to make things happen through a commitment to collaboration. This again links to aspects of COEL for children and provides excellent role modelling.

Confidence

Rodd (2015) recognised that successful teams are characterised by a set of achievable goals which are understood and accepted by all. An OPLC must break down the vision into smaller, achievable sections and tasks to really enhance the involvement of the staff team alongside the inclusion of the community, families and children. The personal views and ideas of the vision become visible through such discussions and can then be drawn together into the professional value system of the setting/school. Sometimes a lack of maturity or experience can lead to teams feeling overwhelmed and unable to move forward. They will be saying 'Tell us what to do.' Creative solutions will need to be found together with sensitive professional development which in turn may take time and negotiation. At other times working alongside a mentor, constructively watching video feedback, providing a non-judgemental sounding board, posing questions, prompting debate and offering inspiration and new experiences will also help. The greatest challenge is finding the time and ideal conditions for these to occur in order to embed the ethos into practice.

Enthusiasm

The focus, energy, enthusiasm and clear communication as an outdoor leader required to develop an OPLC presents both challenges and pleasures. Open and transparent dialogue is a central strategy based upon a sense of ownership where members collaborate and support reflective conversations. The safe environment culture created via non-agenda informal meetings encourages participation and involvement simply through the invitation rather than expectation to participate. It may start with a discussion topic e.g. weather and play or a focus on a particular learning zone outside. Such discussions can then share perceptions, help to determine critical thoughts, find creative solutions and feed naturally into quality improvement as active learners alongside the implementation of policy and procedure whilst leadership learning is taking place at that time too. The related skills of resourcefulness, resilience and reflectivity will also be required to ensure that the enthusiasm is founded on a secure foundation.

Creativity

The concept of an OPLC is a shift from the traditional paradigm of settings and schools. However, many settings and schools are starting to develop a slower culture of shared learning, positive relationships, new ideas and processes in order to achieve their very best for children. The strength of this model of *guardianship of learning* is strongly based in the theorists of early children e.g. Malaguzzi (1993) discussed in Edwards (1995) and far earlier with Froebel in their models of planning for the child and more recently Laevers (1997) in terms of wellbeing and involvement.

Understanding of what children need

Outdoor provision should be based on the children and what they are interested in and need to learn in developmentally appropriate ways. Central to this OPLC is the pedagogical foundation in knowing the children in our care and observing them so we can support their developmental journey effectively. Confident staff understand this pedagogical foundation in the COEL. If everyone understands the principles then the provision of the emotionally secure outdoor learning environment is presented to children in the most effective ways so they can all play and learn. We therefore need to observe closely the children for the 'clues' or possible lines of relevant development to support their particular phase of development. The involvement of families via a key person approach then can offer the genuine depth of relationship with parents to enhance the child's learning and development at home too. The provision of suitable resources can encourage deep level learning through such opportunities with pulleys, loose parts, woodwork, gardening, etc. Allowing babies/children the time and space to free flow in outdoor spaces which are developmentally appropriate and provide suitable risk and challenge will further guarantee quality learning and build confidence over time in dealing with adversity and unpredictability which arise naturally outdoors.

Figure 7.1 Experiences provide rich learning outdoors.

Understanding what adults need

Deciding to take children and the curriculum outdoors is easy, especially if you are aware of the benefits socially, emotionally, physically and cognitively. However great your passion, there will always be someone in your team who is far harder to convince. This can be a huge challenge to other team member's participation as this person can act as a gatekeeper by sharing their reservations. So how do we encourage these reluctant staff to step outside the comfort of the classroom?

Your staff team will vary considerably in their personal experience of the world outside. Some will always prefer indoors, but many will follow a sensitive lead if supported with the provision of appropriate clothing and footwear. Over time they will gradually start to explore and enjoy some of the possibilities. Good starters are a nature table indoors, growing potatoes, minibeast hunts, and feeding the birds. A small steps approach and lots of encouragement and praise are essential. Just like the children, follow an approach of starting where the learner is now alongside liberal encouragement.

One individual in a school/setting can make a positive or negative difference outdoors. Sometimes staff who are not trained can control children's choices through their own fears and concerns. (E.g. lunch time staff or the caretaker.) In other circumstances, the reverse is true where through the involvement and commitment of the outdoor leader modelling experiences and expectations, all staff gain confidence and develop their own practice. Remember that it's not only spoken language but also how body language conveys curiosity, indifference or frustration.

If we see outdoors as threatening then all sorts of fears take over and our inner anxiety transfers to our team, the families and children. Developing an outdoor culture from zero is best done slowly and in small steps by taking folk with you and using the children's development, learning and wellbeing as the driver.

Trust is something which emerges gradually. First, we need to trust ourselves and our abilities. This is aided by high quality training and mentoring. Gradually taking others on board is best achieved through mutual support and celebration in small steps.

For those working beyond the areas of early childhood, the sector can seem very bewildering. In regard to outdoors, some will struggle even more to understand what is happening and will ask:

- Where is the learning?
- Who is in charge?
- What is making a difference to these children?
- What are the expectations, outcomes?
- Are they 'just playing'?

The outdoor leader and their team will grow in confidence and competence over time as their setting/school and community grow together. Showing round a visitor or an inspector gives many opportunities to explain how through play children learn and benefit from being outside.

Knowledge to lead the curriculum outside

The Characteristics of Effective Learning should provide the foundation to the outdoor curriculum whilst ensuring high expectations and developmentally appropriate outcomes through play.

Every day and every experience outdoors should be reflected upon, especially in the early stages, considering curricular aspects which have been highly successful, alongside aspects which need to be improved or even discarded previously.

If we believe that children are our future, then we need to ensure they access the best of experiences indoors and out. If we want them to care for the planet then they have to have opportunities to be a part of it by planting seeds, exploring loose parts, using recycled items creatively, exploring, identifying, wondering and so on.

Opportunities for the children need to be developmentally appropriate to them in all cognitive, physical, social and emotional ways. However, the curriculum provided in every setting and school will be as unique and different as they are.

We need to focus our provision on the Unique Child in early childhood and this leads into the National Curriculum when children are developmentally ready. Each child will vary in experience, confidence and opportunities outdoors so the considerations must be about the following:

- Where is the child now?
- Where do we want them to be?
- How do we get there?
- What provisions in our enabling environment will assist this?
- Which positive relationships will also help?
- How can we enrich learning and development outside?

Linking experiences outdoors to the EYFS and the National Curriculum takes time, skill and experience. Ultimately be patient and encourage.

What it means to lead outdoors

- Talk openly about the benefits of sessions outdoors – it will hook some staff and parents in, even if some remain wary.

Figure 7.2 Experiences which link to developmental phases encourage children to extend their horizons.

- Share what you do and how you do it via displays, newsletters and videos alongside sensitively celebrating the successful steps others in the team are making outdoors alongside those of the children.
- Find out about people's childhood and life experiences outdoors as this is often a sound starting point for next steps. Those that fear the outdoors may have had a traumatic event so will need time, sensitive handling and empathy to heal.
- Remind adults of the feelings of freedom, independence, joy, wonder and fun to be achieved outdoors as central to the values of your setting/school. Build upon this and provide them with opportunities as adults for fun, enjoyment and positive experiences outdoors.

- Use team building experiences such as den building, campfires, mud play, and heuristic play to encourage involvement. Encourage discussion and reflection afterwards.
- Remember, small is beautiful. Often schools and settings with the most outdoor spaces are often the most underused so discuss how you can use the gardening patch, chalk marking on the tarmac, stories, the digging area, the wall, the pond etc. more effectively.
- Less is more should be a central feature. Do not overwhelm adults or children. Take small steps over time and build confidence in one area before moving on so not to overwhelm them.

Provide the best quality resources and support that you can. Staff often lack ideas of what to do with children and resources and are fearful of following their leader if you are not there. Let them observe you or a confident practitioner so they don't stumble at the first hurdle.

Understanding group dynamics outdoors

Group dynamics concerns the formation of groups, along with their structure, processes, and function. The skilful utilisation of group dynamics facilitates constructive changes in children's behaviour and attitudes.

The way groups of people interact affects their decisions. When groups of people work together, the decisions they make result from more than just the decision-making expertise of the individuals. Group dynamics play a critical role in the quality and creativity of their decisions.

What does this look like?

It is known that attitudes are crucial in ensuring a positive ethos outdoors. The following are essential if you wish to ensure children's access to development and learning outdoors.

- Open communication with team members being willing to discuss issues and problems throughout a project.
- Alignment.
- Conflict resolution.
- Commitment to the project.
- Optimistic thinking.

The 4 elements of group dynamics

- Resources, structure (group size, group roles, group norms, and group cohesiveness).
- Processes (communication, group decision-making processes.
- Power dynamics, conflicting interactions, etc.).
- Tasks (complexity and interdependence).

Benefits of team dynamics

- Greater collaboration – greater levels of cooperation are possible when teams work in a more informal and supportive atmosphere.
- Faster decision-making – team members are more willing to listen to each other and so make faster decisions.
- Problem-solving.
- Conflict resolution.
- Shared purpose. The difference between a team and a group is that a team has a shared goal.
- Trust and openness.
- Willingness to correct mistakes.
- Diversity and inclusion.
- Interdependence and a sense of belonging.
- Consensus decision-making.
- Participative leadership and potential successional leadership.

Ensuring successful collaboration

i) Address problems quickly. If you see a team member engaging in unhelpful behaviour, work to address it quickly.

ii) Create a team code of practice to build a positive culture.

iii) Enhance and celebrate team culture.

iv) Build communication.

v) Always pay attention.

vi) Value diversity.

vii) Value relationships.

viii) Make sound appointments to the team.

ix) Establish clear behavioural expectations and hold people accountable.

x) Resolve conflicts.

Delegating and making the most of your team

Those who work outdoors are often very caring, sensitive and nature aware. However, some teams will include folk whose experiences may be more limited but will still be valid. My own experiences of leadership include being very aware of the quietest voice in the room. Thus, we need to be inclusive of all and anyone who wishes to be involved with children outdoors. They all can act as role-models and leaders.

The defining factor behind these folk and those who 'officially' lead outdoors is passion and understanding of children's right to experience outdoors in its varied provisions. This is the true essence of outdoor leadership I believe.

Ideally, these official outdoor leaders should be involved daily outdoors but essentially should empower everyone to maximise experiences, opportunities and provide quality for every child outdoors. These leaders and delegated staff champions will define the ethos and vision of the setting/school and establish clearly agreed guidance about curriculum, pedagogy and assessment outdoors. How confident these practitioners are in their delegated responsibilities will depend upon the trust and respect from their leaders.

Supporting staff and CPD outdoors

All headteachers, leaders and managers should be nurturing staff to value and be involved outdoors. Ideally high-quality professional development and training for all staff should be ongoing, although in these challenging times that can be hard to plan and finance.

- High expectations really do make a difference.
- Celebrating achievements and progress makes for happy quality staff.
- Professional qualifications are a significant factor in determining positive outcomes too.
- An eye on strategic development, investment and extending provision outdoors for older and more confident children is also crucial.

CPD is expensive and demanding but in actual fact many improvements outdoors can happen through teams working together, via mentoring and modelling alongside the children, as well as targeted but reflective staff meetings which focus upon areas for development. Training and professional self-development outside should concentrate upon:

- Being a sensitive consistent practitioner outside who is aware of their posture, body language, voice volume and position, and its effects upon children.
- Children's involvement and interests at different times of the day, week, and in different weathers and seasons – are we making the most of these?
- What the different purposes are for experiences provided outside, what is particularly special on our site and which are we not making the most of?
- The importance of adult visibility and emotional security for children outdoors.
- How to be a play partner or companion with children outdoors.
- How play is the main driver for learning outside and driving the curriculum without any formal planning.
- How to maximise the potential of the outdoor environment through observation and having conversations with children.
- How to interpret and reflect as a team upon children's play, learning and interests to maximum effect.
- How to lead adult-led experiences which build upon observed interests and deep involvements to extend learning and development.
- Filling gaps in our outdoor provision by exploring the local community and finding additional experiences and opportunities.
- Trusting children to lead outdoor learning. To adapt by coining the well-known advertising phrase 'just do it!'

The formal leader is held responsible for quality improvement within their context but through quality staff continuing professional development and regular attention to policies, plans, finance, audits, health and safety etc. Quality improvement is sometimes an area neglected in terms of shared responsibility outdoors but is an excellent way to grow confidence, enthusiasm, knowledge, skills and understanding if effectively delegated amongst a team. By recognising and sharing responsibilities, colleagues gain confidence, prestige and respect. They grow into the roles and responsibilities and are more likely with sensitive support and, where required, training to become outdoor champions and leaders themselves. This helps to build succession in leadership as a direct result.

If we start by considering how education requires educators to support children's ability to learn and think for themselves, we are dealing with a vast array of unknown challenges, complexities and uncertainties. The richer the range of opportunities to grow and extend your learning as an adult, the more likely you are to prosper and grow over time. Thus, by providing small learning steps over time, adults will start to appreciate the fullness of what is being offered and how it can help them in their career. It will also help to nurture trust and self-belief too.

Leading children

As adults we need to see the world through the eyes of young children. A rich and in-depth understanding of play and child development are crucial. As is the first time you see raindrops on a leaf or a frosted cobweb or when you discover potatoes in soil having planted tubers so many months before, these are catalysts for interests, concept formation, language development and the drivers for further exploration. For every child these first-time opportunities can be life changing.

Interests often start with a child spotting and understanding the patterns, colours, print and messages which adorn our local communities. For example: pretending to be a cow, mooing after visiting a farm or being a firefighter after visiting the local fire station. For young children these initial experiences are electrifying and ignite all sorts of learning pathways as they start to build concepts, vocabulary, knowledge, skills and understanding which can last a lifetime. Sensitive adults support and extend their interests and learning outdoors in a wide variety of ways which are in tune with each child. Often this is achieved by being a play partner or companion. Supporting resilience in particular is crucial so that a child develops the ability to deal with adversity, try again, problem-solve, and explore other ways even in the face of difficulties.

Ultimately, for children to learn well outdoors we need to tap into their particular interests, curiosity, fascinations, energy and enthusiasms. Then by collaborating and being able to apply what they have learned, we can support their progress across their holistic development. By reading relevant stories and providing a rich array of both fiction and non-fiction books we can further enrich these initial interests and extend them across the curriculum. For example: Our youngest grandson has always loved being outdoors from a baby. One of his favourite books as a 2-year-old was a small RHS photographic guide to fruits and vegetables. This he chose from a bookshelf once he was crawling. He has gone on to do lots of gardening and particularly likes to harvest fruit and vegetables as he is also a keen eater. He has carefully observed the growth from sowing onwards and learned to recognise different types of apples, pears, berries, tomatoes, carrots, potatoes and beans etc in photographs and then as they have grown and developed in reality. His patience in waiting for the day he can eat them has been peppered by his phrase 'Not ready yet' as he checks them out for readiness. Then when the day came to harvest he couldn't wait to eat some produce, often for the first time with carrots being nibbled straight from the ground. This is lived experience. He has gradually built his concept of ripening too whilst building his trust in us to help him know when to pick and eat these fruits and vegetables.

If we wish to grow outdoor leaders for the future we need to nurture outdoor leadership skills in the children from an early age. To achieve this we can:

Figure 7.3 Observing the child's interests and following them up appropriately.

- Increase children's access to information when they show an interest or ask questions and explain in an age appropriate manner.
- Allow our authority to be questioned.

Allow them to make mistakes, not overreact and support learning from them positively.

Inspire and encourage children to learn in small groups, to collaborate and problem-solve together, to think for themselves and find solutions creatively.

Conclusion

Outdoor leadership is about people and quality involvement and experiences with children. Staff need to be well deployed so that all responsibilities and roles are provided. Their primary understanding of children is achieved by observing and reflecting on the children's play, learning, wellbeing, dispositions and interests.

Outdoor leaders possess the essential qualities, beliefs, knowledge, skills and understanding to provide the life changing experiences which ALL children need and have a right to outdoors. These champions can also sensitively assist team members in gaining the skills, understanding and knowledge to provide excellence outdoors over time. We all **need to approach outdoors with a culture of 'not knowing' and openness** to the vast range of possibilities for play and learning. **Leadership outdoors provides the foundations to the life chances of our children and is central to the provision of high-quality learning and play for babies, children and adults if our planet is to survive.**

Successful schools/settings are underpinned by effective teams who work together and who have an unrelenting focus on improving achievement for all children outdoors often via an OPLC approach. Support for one another, trust, collaboration and reciprocal flexibility to develop and enhance outdoor quality are also crucial. This is not embedded through authority but via influence. So be brave and champion outdoors whatever your role and responsibilities!

8 Leadership beyond the setting/school

Introduction

Future outdoor provision and leadership is essential for building the nature connections we need to understand and deal with the huge challenges facing our planet. We all have a responsibility to develop sustainable schools and settings that respect the world around us and recognise the importance of nature. This chapter considers the next steps in leadership outdoors and how we can ensure that it is sustainable in an uncertain world and how we can continue to grow the important provision outdoors for babies and young children.

Whilst we know that young children are situated within their family as an ecological context, they are also part of their locality, community and ultimately the world. Teaching them about their connectedness and how their actions and those of others have consequences should be framed in growing their values and attitudes of respect rather than as 'saviours' of the planet. Our leadership focus in this chapter concentrates on the community and families working collaboratively. It should include opportunities to nurture empathy and different ways of dealing with issues and problems outdoors.

Celebrating knowledge and understanding whilst building connections outdoors

We need to celebrate and bring in the diversity of indigenous knowledge and understanding from around the world. Countries such as New Zealand and Canada are increasingly building connections with their first nation peoples and the natural environment and finding ways to protect it as land-based education. This movement is based in the fresh air and is grounded in physicality. Through this approach and in valuing cultural roots, we can see ourselves as a part of something

DOI: 10.4324/9780429436505-9

Figure 8.1 Learning to care – (boys cleaning out school pets).

much bigger and part of a world community trying to build strong foundations for a better planet. We can ask questions such as:

- Whose traditional territory are you living on?
- Who lived here before us?
- What's the history of this place?
- How did that history unfold and how did that impact the land and the people?
- What can be done to repair some of the damage?

This may seem far removed from our crowded island but ultimately, we all come from nomadic or land-based cultures if you go far enough back in time, so we have a chance to reconnect with our ancestors and people we may well have forgotten. Whilst we can use technology to help us in this, we can also investigate our local history by, for example, visiting to a records office or church. This may prove very interesting for 6- and 7-year-olds and could lead to further questions such as to where our water or power comes from or how our roads developed locally.

Building connectedness in outdoor communities

Bringing your setting/school closer to its diverse families and local community will help to expand 'social glue,' enhance quality interactions, break down socially constructed barriers and nurture a learning community which values and uses its outdoor provision wisely. Without trust, leadership is unstable, unhappy and lost. Strong communities nurture stronger families and children in many ways such as power sharing, decision-making and productive change. Trust ultimately is a willingness to be vulnerable to the actions of others because we believe they have good intentions and will behave well towards us. Trust is broken when there is limited or no understanding of how a decision was taken alongside a feeling that certain group perspectives have been pushed aside. Community engagement within a school or setting builds trust by allowing group members to interact with decision-makers and provide input. If it is done well, the people feel partners alongside the decision-makers.

There are many ways to build trust via whole school/setting community engagement in outdoor play and learning. For example:

- Starting and continuing meaningful conversations about what you wish to achieve outdoors to gain valuable input and support from all parties.
- Showing you care about others and providing honest and timely feedback in the spirit of wanting people to do better and benefit from being outdoors.
- Taking a genuine interest and remembering the important and sometimes small to life changing things about community members.
- Being transparent by sharing information before, during and after projects and developments.
- Sharing your goals, strengths and weaknesses in simple and clear language to children and families.
- Being consistent in doing what you say you will do via ongoing collaboration, frequently reporting back, and showcasing how you arrived at your decision and why.
- Demonstrating your competence, but also acknowledging your own areas for improvement to show that you don't have to be perfect to excel.
- Being compassionate and treating people kindly. If you genuinely want people to do better and care, it is far easier if you mean it. After all, if others don't trust you, you cannot lead.

Once the locality becomes involved and the wider community 'gets' what you are trying to do for young children, they most often will provide extra benefits and support such as volunteers, plants and seeds, loose parts and resources, funding, external advice and expertise which can all add value. It then becomes a Two-way street with ideas and benefits flowing both ways to the benefit of all.

Ways to support families

There are many ways you can build community trust as a leader in outdoor developments through collaboration and sharing resources and expertise. All of the following can grow individual and cultural confidence, nurture self-esteem and build community cohesiveness if sensitively consulted upon and developed. Sometimes it requires slow learning, close observation and careful choosing of the right moment too. This may include:

- Allowing the community to use your site when the school/setting is closed for local events, celebrations etc. so they too can enjoy the space, freedom and opportunities.
- Building adult understanding, ideas and genuine inclusion by giving them meaningful experiences via involvement in projects e.g. developing a community garden bed or designing something for the outdoor area such as a bird table, creating decorative bunting or den shelter which enhances their skills.
- Building a joint community database of expertise to share when developing structures or creating new seedbeds. Local allotment holders are often keen to help plus groups which involve senior citizens in woodwork, metal work and crafting.
- Mentoring and coaching community representatives on their projects so that they can lead these sessions for themselves.
- Organising joint celebrations and gatherings outside such as picnics in the park, bird watching, spring and autumn events to learn crafts outside.

An effective outdoor learning community will need to ensure the following:

- A learning/play culture which attracts, nurtures and retains its vision for its community of children, families and quality staffing.
- A sensitive approach to the timing and evolution of the outdoor project and how it includes folk.
- A positive, upbeat climate which accepts change as part of life and sees it as a means to nurture new ideas and expand experiences for both adults and children.

- A 'can do culture' which is open and accepting of the community's collective outdoor leadership, careers and futures rather than the growth and success of one individual.
- Investment in terms of time (and ideally money), staff training and bringing in volunteers with useful expertise.
- A value placed on circular economic development that encourages repairing, borrowing and recycling rather than buying.
- Ultimately an acceptance that this means whoever presides over the changes gradually hands over control and reduces their own power and influence. This is subsidiary rather than hierarchical leadership.

The opportunity to give children, families and colleagues the chance to be a part of something important outdoors which they never imagined is immensely empowering. Thus you need to think carefully about your outdoor area in the longer term and how it will continue to benefit children and families. As mentioned, one very obvious way to do this is to open up your outdoor provision and allow community use throughout the year, so it doesn't sit unused during holiday periods. This is quite a challenge but feasible as in the ways children's centres were opened up to a much broader community use with appropriate vision and funding.

Some ways to grow outdoor futures

Ideally, we would celebrate the growth and expansion of outdoor provision first in early childhood as it extends into primary education and then into secondary education as well as whole communities. However, this will take time. In order to grow children into future environmentally aware citizens who are environmentally friendly and economically aware, it is not enough for outdoor leaders to only focus on isolated outdoor experiences. Rather, leaders need to have a critical gaze on what kind of citizens the children are being shaped into through their experiences and how they align with staff who are also connected to nature and outdoors. This means that we need to think about what kind of cultures and values children/adults are coming from and how these relate to their social, emotional and cognitive experiences outdoors. Sometimes joining in may simply be about seeing other folk who look like you and speak your language so role-modelling is crucial too.

We need to carefully reflect on how democratic and diverse these opportunities are for the uniqueness of the children and adults. There are a host of reasons why families might not access your outdoor provision. Some may be highly personal through life experience, others will include more general fears. Ultimately being inclusive must include words, time and actions alongside respect. Basic provision of suitable outdoor clothing for adults and children is a good starting point once they get there. However, some harder to reach families and communities will require extreme sensitivity and consideration including translation provision, joined-up work between different professionals e.g. green prescribing or buddying up with more confident families or groups. For the provision of sound outdoor gear and footwear and its worth trying the charity The Outdoor Guide (https://theoutdoorguide.co.uk) as they are helping schools with this particularly in these challenging times. Some groups may need to be prioritised and grown into using local opportunities such as parks and museums. I have found that taking parent/grandparent volunteers on such opportunities out into the local community actually helps them go back again with far greater confidence. The app https://50thingstodo.org can be very useful here if its available in your area.

Providing opportunities for active experiential learning

Attitudes towards nature, community, climate and the environment vary immensely with weather, mud and concerns about potential accidents often being barriers. We need to build unity, understanding and connectedness by providing accessible, appropriate resources, active pedagogy and real hands-on experiences. This means learning through participation and interactions outdoors (showing how to use dock leaves for nettle stings for example) rather than acquisition from adult-directed agendas. It is not neat and tidy learning but often great fun, messy and unpredictable. It takes time to enculture adults and some children into these but it is a challenge well worth rising to. I recently saw our local day nursery taking all their children to visit a local Chinese restaurant to celebrate Chinese New Year. They had been tasting Chinese food and were now keen to visit a restaurant to support learning. It was a cold and frosty morning so they were all well wrapped up and excited with the youngest in buggies and the older ones accompanied by a good adult/child ratio. I recalled the demands on staff just getting such an expedition organised, then the on the day preparation and finally getting dressed, toileted etc. to go out. The result was a stronger exciting connection to a community restaurant and an opportunity to walk on a cold day with a purpose. Children also were challenged by tasting different food which some of them had never experienced before and understanding that trying different foods is often a great opportunity. Back in the nursery they were able to role-play restaurants too.

Challenge and self-chosen challenge are really important for children as it leads to both a depth and breadth of potential learning. Researchers Coates and Pimlott-Wilson (2019) interviewed 33 children from 2 mainstream primary schools in England who had recently completed a 6-week Forest School programme. Their analysis revealed 3 inter-related themes: a break from routine; learning through play; collaboration and teamwork. The findings suggest that the blending of Forest School with mainstream settings contributes to children's social, cognitive, emotional and physical skill development through experiential learning using play. These findings are significant because they not only emphasise the values of social constructivist play-pedagogy which underpin Forest School practice, but also highlight the need for primary schools to consider learning outside of the classroom as an effective pedagogy by providing the best environment in their local area for children to explore and be adventurous when compared to the indoor classroom.

I often use the example of an apple as a great example of experiential learning. I compare it with a plastic role-play apple to encourage folk to see the vast learning potential of a real apple. If you add more real apples, you add more variety and the potential of more holistic and specific learning e.g. colour, shape, size, smell, and number before starting to explore the apple by cutting it up to explore taste, fractions, plus vertical and horizontal perspectives. The latter provides the magical opportunity of seeing the star shape of the pips too! This learning exploration can be taken a stage further by examining a real apple tree and its context by being there in its habitat. Try to revisit this tree across the seasons to record its changes by drawing, painting and photographing it to build further curricular possibilities. Thus, children learn about the world around them starting small and familiar but extend their learning by partaking meaningfully in the world around them at their pace rather than being fed it top down in a traditional 'one size fits all' fashion.

Just do it! Experiential learning in practice A reminder of where to start is important in terms of families and communities. Recognising where they are from, what their culture, religion, ethnicity and life experiences can all play a part in their lives and thus are central to finding your starting point with them. Place and space are important considerations when planning contextual experiences for immersion in the community and nature. A tarmac space is not always the most inspirational but by growing a few fruits, vegetables and flowers in containers, a transformation starts to occur where nature starts to impact on the learning possibilities and fascinations. This is also a great example of a circular economic approach. Other contextual experiences and potential challenges include:

- Exploring through touch.
- Growing food and cooking what you harvest and helping budgets.
- Shopping, bus and train trips and community involvement in events.
- Experiencing the elements and seasonal change in the same place over time.
- Giving names to spaces and features which interest them such as the 'crocodile log' which create a home connection as well as a reference point on a walk.
- Learning the correct biological names of plants and animals.
- Observing and reflecting upon the web of life, life and death, beauty, awe and wonder and developing a spiritual understanding of outdoors.
- Physically responding to different obstacles and moving items such as a fallen tree, snow and ice.

- Sensory opportunities such as listening to bird song, sliding in mud, looking at wood rotting.

We need to continue to convince the whole of society that being outdoors is great for everyone's health and wellbeing, and disconnecting from technological devices for periods of time may assist in the process of making learning stick. The learning is more memorable and the experience is more stimulating and therefore it is retained.

Nurturing real learning connections for life Children need to be prepared for the future world and that means providing them with opportunities that support their creativity and their technical knowledge. A simple short walk will avail the children of some fascinations such as drain covers, gate hinges, door numbers, post box etc. These local explorations are often overlooked in terms of the understanding developed of simple scientific and technological concepts such as levers, hydraulics. There are also clear links to mathematics, communication, language and literacy and the humanities. Following up such walks with stories back at the setting or school as well as loaning them to families can add real educational value. The careful use of simple questions after observations can guide possible next steps too. Investing in a few jeweller's loupes (eye piece magnifiers) to investigate the tiny things, which young children are expert at finding can also provoke immense fascination.

In a multi-sensory environment such as a local wood or park, inner emotional boundaries can be better experienced and expressed. Our 2.5-year-old grandchild has named a wooded copse in our local park as 'the foggy, foggy forest' after reading the Nick Sharratt story with the same title, and by recognising some of its features from this favourite story. This growing sense of place provides familiarity and ownership through a child's play, making their strengths perceptible and their confidence and understanding of boundaries more evident and valued. This can lead to a 'flow state' which is a great sign of learning as it indicates that the individual is immersed and concentrating deeply in something which fascinates them. Simple wildlife guides can be a great resource (The Woodland Trust and Field Studies Council sell a great selection.).

Interconnectedness and inclusion If we want to help children to become caretakers of our planet we first need to help them love and understand it. This starts with broad open-ended, inclusive thinking to provide rich opportunities for all children in the community. By getting the provision outdoors the best it can be for every unique child, then it is far more effective as a learning environment for all. This means really getting to know our children and families so we can take on board their life experiences, their interests and needs.

By looking to include <u>all</u> children we create a very powerful model of success. Thus we must start by consulting children about what they use, how they use it, what they enjoy or don't enjoy outdoors. Some features for example will extend their physical opportunities whilst others extend their social play. If we can reflect upon how the environment affords risky, thrilling and adventurous play alongside the benefits of being in nature then further opportunities will be available. This can be helped by proving opportunities to:

- Giving children the opportunity to take responsibility for caring for an area outside e.g. tidying up.
- Looking after particular plants and knowing what they particularly need in terms of care.
- Buddying up with a new child or a child with SEND as a good role-model.
- Counting how many children have accessed snack provision and cleaning the area when it ends.
- Recording simple data e.g. bird table visitors, seedling growth.

Inclusion of all children should be at the forefront of our thinking and planning about what to do and where to go outside. So children who are fascinated by the trajectories of planes may benefit from exploring more about birds, feathers, balls, kites and paper darts for example. Others may be fascinated by minibeasts, so a hunt under logs and stones will provide great opportunities for discovery and enrichment with simple identification guides. If we start with the child's observed interests and fascinations then regardless of their unique needs and circumstances we can both include them, value them and often help them in leading other children's learning too. Adapting the environment, the resources, provisions such as clothing, staffing, transportation etc. may also be essential for genuine inclusion. Alongside this we need to be mentally flexible and adaptable in how we approach children's interests especially if these involve active engagement and excited curiosity so we can mediate for these more physically demanding learning approaches.

This interconnectedness can also build upon cultural understanding from previous generations and ancestors. This can start simply through parents, grandparents and community members reading stories and skill sharing via gardening, cookery, woodwork, arts and crafts, construction and photography. Special events like bring your Dad/Grandparent to school day also work well as well as sharing multi-cultural festivals. Learning to share our world and its riches is an important starting point and many cultures have a rich history of such connectedness we should value. Whilst a Headteacher, we built strong connections with the Royal Hospital, Chelsea. These gentlemen having been Disclosure and Baring Service checked loved the opportunity to talk and learn with the children as often they had no family themselves. One played the piano, another the drums whilst one helped with gardening and another sat telling stories to a group of enrapt youngsters. Being outside together as a community also provides rich opportunities to demonstrate the values of diversity. Whilst diversity cannot be taught, we can show how it is a normal, natural and enriching part of everyday life via such opportunities as music, cooking and gardening. These processes are all about watering, weeding, creating, measuring, mixing and making and often begin via the seeds that are metaphorically planted in our outdoor walks and journeys. Without such care and attention, the plants (children/adults) will not flourish outdoors.

By providing such wonderful opportunities through the leadership outdoors for children and families, we are creating stronger community engagement and relationships. We know that research confirms that natural environments promote relaxation and use of the imagination whilst developing cognitive, social and emotional skills and capabilities in children. However, it is the co-operation and involvement of other partners such as parents, grandparents and volunteers which extend the synergies still further into their lives.

Community projects

As children are all unique we also need to provide a rich range of affordances (Gibson, 1979) in their opportunities to play and learn outside. We need to reflect carefully on what, where and how we offer opportunities to explore outdoors without further damaging our world through waste or creating false roles for them to follow. Many settings and schools are finding local support for the exploration of local outdoor spaces. I have had the privilege of volunteering on such a community project at the Holy Brook Nook in Reading and seen classes of quite vulnerable children grow in confidence, understanding and skills in being outdoors.

These experiences act as doors, windows and skylights for children to explore a small part of their locality. In just a few weeks they know the golden rules of staying safe, how to transport sticks, make seed bombs, identify birds, small mammals and minibeasts and have generally become very much more observant of the world around them.

What is clear is that different locations from large to small provide different affordances and lead to different play and learning for young children. By using the concept of place-based education Wally Penetito (2009) focussed upon connectedness and unity of education with its local area and community. This is the context for learning and provides a venue for children to take responsibility for and have attachment to their surrounding area. This builds positive affiliation and connections gradually over time with adults and older children acting as role-models and guides for new starters. Older, more confident children seem to particularly enjoy being more independent and finding hiding places away from adults.

Leading for sustainability – how do we want them to learn about these issues?

While we want young children to know that earth is our home and that it is important to respect and care for the environment, it's not appropriate to give them the burden of saving it. If we catastrophise we risk frightening them to such a degree that they will give up feeling that re-engaging with planet earth is hopeless and overwhelming.

Outdoors provides a positive warp and weft for the enrichment of aspects of curriculum alongside an understanding of sustainability. For example mathematics is advanced by increasing spatial awareness, measurement and number bonds, and schemas, categorisation, problem solving and creative active thinking which all help to build foundations for science, history, geography, and expressive arts particularly via children's own questions and fascinations. Social learning outdoors meanwhile feeds into wellbeing, language, communication and literacy. The learning children experience outside will become evident over time through the concepts they understand, skills they've reinforced and mastered. A child aged 30 months can quickly learn to distinguish and recognise via hands-on opportunities the differences between a holly tree, fir tree and monkey puzzle tree, alongside understanding that they are all prickly to a greater or lesser degree.

Ecophobia or a fear of potential damaging environmental issues can be created in children causing far more harm than good. However, involving them in nature, sustainability and re-engagement with nature is essential as a recent report by United Nations Educational, Scientific and Cultural Organisation (UNESCO Digital Library) (2015), which demonstrates many positives. This report, 'The Contribution of Early Childhood Education to a Sustainable Society,' clearly describes how the understandings, attitudes, values and habits acquired during the early years can have a long-lasting impact on children, society and the natural environment. The report calls for a 'new kind of education' that recognises the important place early years education has 'in the efforts to bring about sustainable development' (UNESCO, 2008, p. 8).

Nurturing sustainability here and now and into the future

So it seems we have a dilemma in how much to involve young children and how pedagogically to teach them about our rapidly changing world. However, this is perhaps no different to many of life's dilemmas. When we look at outdoor play and learning, outdoors provides an environment which is the 'third teacher' (Wurm, 2005). The core in experiential learning is that children learn about the world by partaking in it rather than reading about it. For example, by examining, drawing and photographing a local tree in its current habitat rather than reading about it. In this way children learn about the context the tree lives in by being a part of the same context. Experiential learning may be summed up by the famous paraphrase of John Dewey: *'learning by doing.'* When we think of experiential learning as learning by doing, many people associate it with practical learning and some sort of activity as a tool for learning in a school/setting. In such a context, learning by doing will likely occur during outdoor play or physical activity in environments outside the classroom.

In another report, however, Natural England (Dillon & Lovell, 2022: Links between natural environments, learning and health: evidence briefing. Natural England Evidence Information Note. EIN063) stress that there is now a great need for further research across a broader sector because most of the evidence continues to relate to children of school age. While a significant number of high-quality studies and reviews have been carried out, there are still too many studies which are short-term and relatively small scale, and which do not adjust for confounders and sources of bias. There is still a need for more focused evidence for particular population subgroups, outcomes, and delivery approaches, although this has improved since the original briefing was published.

Young children are quick to understand that you can buy vegetables wrapped in plastic in shops but you can also grow them yourself. This initially helps them understand aspects of waste, gardening, alongside circular economics and logistics as they are older. Adults teach children in many unspoken ways, so as caregivers we should ensure that our actions and behaviours coincide with our words in order to nurture positive understanding of our rapidly changing world.

With climate and environmental change one of the world's largest issues today our children will need to solve complex problems or face unknown consequences. They will sadly bear the brunt of its damaging effects. Thus education for sustainable development is critical and settings/schools are an excellent place to start. This may lead to uncomfortable questions as to people's desire (or lack of desire) to make sustainable choices. Saving the planet will not simply happen because children play outdoors. Nor will it happen with the best plans for successional outdoor leadership. There needs to be far more pedagogical awareness alongside stopping seeing young children as too developmentally immature and in need of overprotection from certain facts about climate change etc. Research by Elliott, Arlemalm-Hagser, and Davis (2020) and Engdahl (2015) indicates if children engage in sustainability they can act upon the knowledge they gain leading to positive transformations in both pedagogy and adult attitudes towards young children's capabilities.

Interactive learning is a powerful link to children's curiosity so try some of these experiences:

- Growing and harvesting vegetables and fruit. Examining the whole plant including the roots, leaves and stems. By growing things from scratch children start to understand and appreciate the time and effort it takes to grow food as it doesn't magically appear on the shelves of supermarkets.
- Develop ways for children to recycle, reuse, decay and compost. Spend time exploring and demonstrating what goes where.
- Examine soil and its constituent parts by placing different soils in bottles of water, shaking and allowing to settle.

- Consider carrying out a simple traffic survey to collect data passing your setting/school. Use the collected data to discuss its possible effects on nature and ourselves. Link it up to walking programmes.

What does an outstanding sustainable outdoor provision look like?

The outdoor environment is the place where children make meaningful connections with the world around them. A key aspect of education for sustainability is creativity, thinking differently and being solution focused. Young children need to be asked the 'What if?', 'I wonder', 'What do you think?' questions and challenges. The diversity of spaces, resources and materials cannot be created indoors easily so outdoors has a head start in sustainability terms. There are some fundamental principles of sustainability which we need to ensure:

- Placing inclusion at the centre of your equality of opportunity policy and practice for all children and ensuring particularly that those with very little experience outdoors gain more time and opportunities outside.
- Valuing diversity and the involvement of a wider range of backgrounds, ethnicities and cultures by involving community representation, by growing a wider range of foodstuffs and linking stories and non-fiction to the outdoor experiences. Often parents and grandparents will share simple recipes, demonstrate cooking and bring in different foodstuffs to share if diets permit.
- Having plenty of loan outdoor gear easily available for supply staff and families in order to access the outdoors.
- Providing genuine capacity to make changes and being involved in the processes of change by being consulted in developments however small by asking regularly how your outdoor provision can be more useful and accessible to them, paying particular attention to babies and those with SEND.
- Understanding our interdependence with the world around us and our nature connectedness through chances to see: food chains for example. Trying to find out the story of a banana or a potato for example.
- Explaining rights and responsibilities alongside adjusting expectations to facilitate greater involvement and participation by all to reflect age, phase, background etc. by developing simple positive rules together.
- Thinking things through before establishing new experiences by ensuring the necessary precautions for possible hazards and uncertainties are dealt with properly such as litter pickers not bare hands.
- Facilitating contributions and ideas from staff and volunteers whilst reflecting upon what actions, adjustments and approaches need to be taken outside whilst . . . .

- Preparing and supporting staff via ongoing quality professional development, mentoring and 1–1 support if required.

Therefore children will need opportunities outdoors to:

- Learn about habitats, plants, wildlife and how these are interlinked with biodiversity and circular economics.
- Learn about how plants have been used safely in the past and how we can continue to use them e.g. fruit tree planting, making compost, felting, blackberrying etc.
- Recycling, permaculture, gardening, reusing items as loose parts in play.
- Being responsible members of a community and engaging in local projects.

Outdoor learning is not an extra to be fitted into education but part of life and all our futures. If we can stress the huge benefits of moving learning from primarily 2D indoors to 3D outdoors then we will gain more support from families, colleagues and society. The wider the community partnerships we build, the broader the demographics and cultures we include resulting in concrete changes and actions will pave the way for future progress. This systematic inclusion of outdoor learning into daily provision is also a very effective means of reducing inequities in children's access to outdoors and thus is a very promising means of looking after our planet.

What do we want young children to learn about sustainability?

We need to try to ensure that all learners acquire the knowledge and skills needed to promote sustainable development and sustainable lifestyles. We also need to reflect upon how we can also teach appropriately about areas such as: human rights, gender equality, promotion of a culture of peace and non-violence, global citizenship and appreciation of cultural diversity and of culture's contribution to sustainable development. This is a base of responsible learning which is underpinned by simple sustainable changes of practices with settings and schools. I recently saw some excellent 'hands-on' training for staff to learn how to make baby wipes from kitchen towel rather than the non-sustainable versions sold over the counter. This small nursery chain was also encouraging recyclable practices with food, nappies etc.

Finally use research to support your case as is demonstrated in Learning Outside the Classroom in Natural Environments (LINE) November 2022) which Natural England illustrate in their recent report demonstrates in relation to primary education that LINE is making a difference to the lives of children across a wide range of primary school settings. The forecast Social Return on Investment (SROI) ratio for learning outside the classroom in natural environment is **£4.32 for every £1 invested**.

The future of our planet should be the greatest concern in our lives. Elliott and Davis (2009) recognised that engaging children in learning about sustainability was and is essential, even at the younger ages. However, there is also evidence alongside them learning about sustainability that multi-level systemic transformational changes across the world are required in society, education and care. Young children are competent and capable of understanding the complexity of the problems but worryingly are not being supported in their educational and care experiences by an adult world which is either over protected, ill-informed or sadly simply not willing to make substantial changes itself (Caiman & Lundegard, 2014; Harwood, 2019; Elliott, Arlemalm-Hagser, & Davis, 2020).

Sustainability goals

There is an increasing awareness of the climate emergency in society as schools and settings are establishing ways to help such as recycling. The 'particular urgency' of COP 26 and 27 alongside what we see reported in the media should be making us more likely to establish greener and 'climate-friendly' life standards and expectations on society. Whilst most Local Authorities, schools and child care businesses are aware of their responsibilities and may try to bring sustainability to the fore of early childhood education, they simply have too many pressures on them. Many have brought in practices such as 'real' nappies and a glitter ban, but how many actually teach children the UNESCO (2015) 17 Sustainable Development Goals (SDGs)? The COEL (DfE, 2021) stress the need for young children to be engaging in learning which includes questioning, thinking and investigation skills. These educational goals marry up to the SDGs which in turn underpin the aims of the Eco-Schools Green Flag accreditation (www.eco-schools.org.uk) which aims to achieve 'net zero' emissions by 2030 alongside more sustainable travel choices.

The SDG are about learning about our responsibilities and need for urgent engagement in taking much better care of our planet in order to reduce climate change etc. OMEP UK's Early Childhood Sustainable Citizenship Award (www.omep.org.uk/esc/) has a child-centred approach to habitats and economic circularity via conservation. Getting young children and their families to embrace their responsibilities to the planet is not 'green washing' but the means to start to change futures. 'Sustainability Matters in Early Childhood' contains numerous ideas, activities, and experiences that promote the 'creativity and curiosity' of young children to take steps towards a greener future by engaging with the Sustainable Development Goals. It was developed by Dr. Diane Boyd, J. King, S. Mann, and J. Neame (2022) and is a free and useful resource which aligns itself with the government's sustainability and climate change strategy for education and children's services systems.

The initiative relates to learning and play outdoors through a series of 'I care' booklets and picture storybooks looking at:

- Nature.
- The causes and impacts of climate change.
- The importance of sustainability.

Once a child has completed an area of 'I care,' they get a sticker for their ECS C passport and recognition for the Early Childhood Sustainability Award at bronze, silver and gold levels. Each child, family and setting work together to complete educational activities that range from the identification and naming of 3 wild birds, the identification of wildlife habitats, to the recycling of waste materials and the recognition of cultural and linguist diversity. The approach states that children must be provided with practical opportunities to 'increase climate resilience, reduce carbon impact and enhance biodiversity,' which will enable them to take positive action to improve their community and their planet.

Other opportunities Start simply with something that is in your direct control, that you have the time and energy to deal with and which is accessible, economically viable and doable, such as LED lighting, food waste, non-toxic cleaning products, and plastic free environments which are all powerful. Make small investments in:

- Auto-off taps.
- Reduced flush cisterns.
- Eco nappies and wipes.
- Aerating taps.
- LED lights.
- Specialist collection and recycling for disposable nappy waste to avoid landfill.
- Solar panels and renewable energy sources.
- Natural insulation using sheep wool.
- Repurposing and recycling resources e.g. mud kitchens.
- Moving away from tacky by trying to bring in longer lasting quality investment in wooden toys, furniture.
- Joining a scrap store.

It is also well worth investigating the following for further ideas:

- https://leyf.org.uk/news/leyf-launches-new-level-4-sustainability-qualification-for-early-childhood-education/

- www.eyalliance.org.uk/news/2021/09/new-alliance-publication-helps-settings-embed-social-responsibility-early-years
- www.flourishproject.net/sdgs-for-the-early-years.html

Leading the leaders

We need to be brave and bold by celebrating and standing up for young children's rights to have developmentally appropriate education and care outside, not the pushed down curriculum of their older peers, who also might incidentally learn far more outside! Activities involving recycling, gardening and caring for the planet fit in naturally to the ways young children learn and become life-long habits. Getting the senior leadership team on board in valuing outdoor learning is often the greatest challenge for any staff member who wants to improve children's access to outdoors. Once you've raised their awareness through the benefits of thriftiness and saving money, they are often far more receptive to other ideas involving pedagogical practice and outdoor curriculum. This often requires a change of culture over sadly sometimes considerable time and may not occur until there are staff changes.

Approaches to getting other leaders to sign up to outdoor play and learning

Sometimes evidence, data, behaviours and holistic approaches will help get your desired outdoor messages out there to those with power, influence and funding. These can include:

- Show how the whole curriculum can be accessed outdoors based upon your knowledge of the children you know and work with, their development and needs as part of 'real school' learning.
- Develop a simple research project or case study collecting data on children's progress when they go outside frequently and regularly.
- Words matter! So start calling it risky learning, daring or adventurous learning which satisfies a child's desire for self-chosen challenges and links to many important aspects of your 3D curriculum.
- Be a playful person who values outdoors by changing perceptions of what play and learning are, what it feels like, what it looks like and is for.
- Make clear links to the United Nations Rights of the Child and the Sustainable Development Goals.
- Look for what brings children and adults into the garden/outdoor area at different seasons and times of day and maximise them.

- Link up with other local settings/schools to discover how they got things moving outdoors and overcame the reticence of the Senior Leadership Team.
- Encourage donations and recycling resourcefulness whilst celebrating circular economies.

You may feel very alone with restrictions placed in your way at every turn. You may need to become the long-playing recording and keep saying the same things sprinkled with some occasional magic and supporting data. It is only when these barriers start to be removed with support at all levels from families, colleagues, SLT, management, Local Authority, Ofsted and society that outdoor learning will become sustainable and will be included in accepted and valued pedagogical practice. However, until then it is worth fighting for as a means to support the next generation and human inhabitation and coexistence on our planet.

What does your environment really offer children? Finally, we need to think about what our environment offers our children. The most important thing you can do is involve the children in as much sustainable practice as you can. Focus on getting them to ask questions and find out their own answers as they take part in both planned and spontaneous activities. Children as you know, will copy your every move whether you want them to or not. Therefore you need to be conscious of how you are treating the environment around you too in order to create a snowball effect. Ask yourself:

Are we as a setting/school?

- Recycling.
- Reusing/repurposing.
- Using less.
- Using our green fingers.
- Considering our buying practices such as bulk or more sustainable choices.
- Conserving water, power and energy.
- Involving families and our community.

Through regular audits linked to statutory documents you can identify gaps and record progress in your provision considering:

- Do all staff demonstrate clear curiosity and joy when being outside?
- Are we demonstrating sustainable practices as in the SDGs?
- How does the environment empower children's learning?

- Do children know where and how they can find out more?
- Do the children have opportunities to care for plants, wildlife, pets etc.?
- Where are the gaps in resources and experiences as well as knowledge, skills and understanding?
- Embracing risk and challenge and building RBA into your core teaching and codes of behaviour.
- Have outdoor playdates and events for families to come and join in to build and strengthen relationships and enhance community unity and connectedness.
- Get volunteers police checked to enhance your adult/child ratios so you can go out more into your local environment.
- Make friends with other staff in local schools and settings to learn from them and how they manage their manager to lead learning outdoors.
- Arrange to meet in each other's outdoor environment and share good practice after hours or on a Saturday morning perhaps?
- Research small grants and funding sources for environmental development and training such as from Learning Through Landscapes, OPAL and environmental charities such as the RSPB and the Woodland Trust., plus Seeds of Change in Scotland.
- Approach local firms and businesses for real hands-on help and resources.
- If you've got something to be proud of flaunt it, share and invite MPs and the media to come and see it.

You cannot teach social and emotional skills and understanding in a vacuum. Children need real experiences to nourish their connection with nature and the planet. We need to grow confident and happy children who understand their lifelong responsibilities. We can start by expecting the following as the basic norm within schools and settings:

i) A culture of courtesy, gratitude, honesty, respect and trust.

ii) A place where we talk about relationships, feelings and emotions to grow understanding and empathy.

iii) Accepting that despite their young age and developmental immaturity, we must teach young children about the state of the environment and how we must make equitable use and take sustainable care of its resources now.

iv) An understanding of how being outside can benefit mental and physical health and how in return we must become caretakers of our planet now before it is too late.

Conclusion – leading outdoors to create better futures for us all

We live in an age where many of the current methods of educating children and young people are not working, so we need to look for alternatives. Ultimately then we must ask the question what do we do next in outdoor learning? The future is about slowing down, reducing pressures, capacity building and growing more grassroots confidence in the benefits, value and gains for human beings and the future of our planet. Whilst the future of our planet looks increasingly challenging, every young child's self-driven curiosity and right is to go out to enjoy and explore nature in their own community. This should be a new driver to ensuring a better and kinder world which we all need to value, respect and harness. So encouraging playing outside from babies onwards is an important first step on a lifelong journey.

Leading learning outdoors bibliography

Allen, G. (2011). *Early Intervention: The Next Steps, an Independent Report to Her Majesty's Government*. London: Cabinet Office.

Alme, H., & Alvestad-Reime, M. (2021). Nature kindergartens: A space for children's participation. *Journal of Outdoor and Environmental Education, 24*(2), 113–131.

Änggård, E. (2009). Making use of "nature" in an outdoor preschool: Classroom, home and fairyland. *Children, Youth and Environments, 20*, 4–25. https://doi.org/10.7721/chilyoutenvi.20.10004.

Anggard, E. (2010). Making use of "nature" in an outdoor preschool: Classroom, home and fairyland. *Children, Youth and Environments, 20*(1), 4–25. Available at www.colorado.edu/journals/cye.

Appleton, J. (1975). *The Experience of Landscapes*. London: John Wiley & Sons.

Athey, C. (1990). *Extending Thought in Young Children: A Parent-Teacher Partnership*. London: Paul Chapman.

Aubrey, C. (2007). *Leading and Managing in the Early Years*. London: Sage.

Avolio, B. J., & Bass, B. M. (2004). *Multifactor Leadership Questionnaire. Manual and Sampler Set* (3rd ed.). Redwood City, CA: Mind Garden.

Bandura, A. (1977). *Social Learning Theory*. New York: Prentice-Hall.

Bandura, A. (1997). *Self-Efficacy: The Exercise of Control*. New York: WH Freeman.

Bareham, J. (2011). *Hidden Gardens of the Royal Mile*. Musselburgh: Greenyonder Tours.

Bartone, P., Eid, J., Johnson, B. J., Laberg, J. C., & Snook, S. (2009). Big five personality factors, hardiness, and social judgement as predictors of leader performance. *Leadership & Organization Development Journal, 30*(6), 498–521.

Beames, S., Higgins, P., & Nicol, R. (2012). *Learning Outside the Classroom* (1st ed., pp. VII–24). N.P.: Routledge.

Benford, M., & Ingham, A. (1987, March 6). Another leap forward. *The Times Educational Supplement*.

Bento, G., & Dias, G. (2017, September–October). The importance of outdoor play for young children's healthy development. *Porto Biomedical Journal, 2*(5).

Bentsen, P., Schipperijn, J., & Jensen, F. S. (2013). Green space as classroom: Outdoor teachers' use, preferences and eco-strategies in relation to green space. *Landscape Research, 39*(5), 561–575.

Berghoefer, U., Rozzi, R., & Jax, K. (2010). Many eyes on nature: Diverse perspectives in the Cape Horn Biosphere Reserve and their relevance for conservation. *Ecology and Society*, *15*(1).

Bilton, H. (2002). *Outdoor Play in the Early Years*. London: David Fulton.

Bilton, H., Bento, G., & Dias, G., (2017). *Taking the First Steps Outside-Under Threes Leaning and Developing in the Natural Environment*. Abingdon: Routledge.

Blanchet-Cohen, N., & Elliot, E. (2011). Young children and educators-engagement and learning outdoors: A basis for rights-based programming. *Early Education & Development*, 759–769.

Boyd, D., King, J., Mann, S., & Neame, J. (2022). *NCSF Sustainability Matters in Early Childhood*. Liverpool John Moores University. Available at www.ncfe.org.uk/media/p1socs4v/sustainability-matters-in-early-childhood-resource.pdf.

Breiting, S., & Wickenberg, P. (2010, February 17). The progressive development of environmental education in Sweden and Denmark. *Environmental Education Research*, 13–16.

Breunig, M. (2019). Beings who are becoming: Enhancing our social justice literacy. *The Journal of Experimental Education*, *42*(1), 7–21.

Bruce, T. (1997). *Early Childhood Education*. London: Hodder and Stoughton.

Bruce, T. (2012). *Early Childhood Practice Froebel Today*. London: SAGE.

Brussoni, M., Gibbons, R., Gray, C., Ishikawa, T., Sandseter, E. B. H., Bienenstock, A., Chabot, G., Fuselli, P., Herrington, S., Jannssen, I., Pickett, W., Power, M., Stanger, N., Sampson, M., & Tremblay, M. (2015). What is the relationship between risky outdoor play and health in children? A systematic review. *International Journal of Environmental Research and Public Health, 12*.

Brussoni, M., Olsen, L. L., Pike, I., & Sleet, D. A. (2012, August 30). Risky play and children's safety: Balancing priorities for optimal child development. *International Journal of Environmental Research and Public Health*, *9*(9), 3134–3148. https://doi.org/10.3390/ijerph9093134. PMID: 23202675; PMCID: PMC3499858.

Buchan, N. (2016). *A Practical Guide to Nature-Based Practice*. London: Bloomsbury.

Bundy, A., Engelen, L., Wyver, S., Tranter, P., Ragen, J., Bauman, A., Baur, L., Schiller, W., Simpson, J. M., Niehues, A. N., Perry, G., Jessup, G., & Naughton, G. (2017). Sydney playground project: A cluster-randomized trial to increase physical activity, play, and social Skills. *Journal of School Health*, *87*(10), 751–759.

Burke, A., & Crocker, A. (2020). "Making waves": How young learners connect with their natural world through third spaces. *Education Sciences*, *10*(8), 203.

Caiman, C., & Lundegard, I. (2014). Pre-school children's agency in learning for sustainable development. *Environmental Education Research*, *20*(4), 437–459.

Carson, R. (1956 reprinted 1965). *The Sense of Wonder*. Harper Collins, 1998 published posthumously.

Caxton, G. (2008). *What's the Point of School? Rediscovering the Heart of Education*. One World Publications, BLP.

Central Advisory Council for Education. (1967). *Children and Their Primary Schools* ("The Plowden Report"). London: HMSO.

Ceppi, G., & Zini, M. (1998). *Children, Spaces, Relations: Meta-Project for an Environment for Young Children*. Modena, Italy: Grafiche Rebecchi Ceccarelli.

Chang, Yuan-Yu, & Chang, Chun-Yen. (2018, February). *The Benefits of Outdoor Activities for Children with Autism*. Corpus.

Charles, E. (1994). New futures at whose cost? In R. Boot, J. Lawrence, and J. Morris (Eds.) *Managing the Unknown by Creating New Futures*. McGraw Hill.

Clark, A. (2023). *Slow Knowledge and the Unhurried Child*. Abingdon: Routledge.

Claxton, G. (2002). *Building Learning Power: Helping Young People Become Better Learners*. Bristol: TLO.

Claxton, G. (2004). Learning to learn: A ley hoal in a 21st century curriculum. *A Discussion Paper for QCA*. London: QCA.

Coates, J. K., & Pimlott-Wilson, H. (2019). Learning while playing: Children's forest school experiences in the UK. *British Educational Research Journal*, *45*(10), 21–40.

Cobb, E. (1977). *The Ecology of Imagination in Childhood*. New York: Columbia University Press.

Constable, K. (2014). *Bringing the Forest School Approach to Your Early Years Practice*. Abingdon: Routledge.

Cooper Marcus, C., & Sachs, N. A. (2013). *Therapeutic Landscapes: An Evidenced Based Approach to Designing Healing*. New Jersey, USA: John Wiley and Sons.

Cunliffe, A. L., & Eriksen, M. (2011). Relational leadership. *Human Relations*, *64*(11), 1425–1449. https://doi.org/10.1177/0018726711418388.

Cutts, E. (2019). *The Dear Wild Place*. Paisley, Scotland: CCWB Press.

Dame Clare Tickell. (2010). Tickell review of the early years foundation stage. DERA Department for Education.

Davis, G., & Ryder, G. (2016). *Leading in Early Childhood*. London: Sage.

Davy, A. (2019). *A Sense of Place-Mindful Practice Outdoors*. London: Featherstone.

DCSF. (2007). *Statutory Early Years Framework (Learning and Development Requirements)*. HMSO.

DCSF (Department for Children, Schools and Families). (2009a). *Learning Outside the Classroom* [Online]. Available at www.dcsf.gov.uk/everychildmatters/ete/school/learningotc.

DCSF (Department for Children, Schools and Families). (2009b). *Learning, Playing and Interacting: Good Practice in the Early Years Foundation Stage*. Department for Children, Schools and Families.

DEFRA. Available at www.google.com/search?client=safari&rls=en&q=People+and+Nature+Survey+2000+RSPB+2021&spell=1&sa=X&ved=2ahUKEwiW3PS4mqHyAhVz-RUEAHcLtC9gQBSgAegQIARAw&biw=1359&bih=726.

Department for Education and Skills. (2007). *Statutory Framework for the Early Years Foundation Stage*. Nottingham: DfES Publications 00013-2007BKT-EN. Available at www.teachernet.gov.uk/publications. Outdoors for All – www.naturalengland.org.uk/ourwork/enjoying/outdoorsforall/diversityreview.

The Desirable Learning Outcomes. (1996). Available at https://assets.publishing.service.gov.uk/government/uploads/system/uploads/attachment_data/file/516537/The_early_years_foundation_stage_review_report_on_the_evidence.pdf.

DfE. *The Tickell Review*. Available at www.gov.uk/government/publications/the-early-years-foundations-for-life-health-and-learning-an-independent-report-on-the-early-years-foundation-stage-to-her-majestys-government.

DfE. (2008). *Early Years Foundation Stage: Statutory Framework*. Department for Education.

DfE. (2012). *Statutory Framework for the Early Years Foundation Stage*. Department for Education.

DfE. (2021). *Development Matters: Non-Statutory Curriculum Guidance for the Early Years Foundation Stage*. Available at https://assets.publishing.service.gov.uk/government/uploads/system/uploads/attachment_data/file/988004/Development_Matters.pdf.

DfES. (2004). *Every Child Matters*. Department for Education and Skills.

DfES. (2006). *Learning Outside the Classroom Manifesto*. Nottingham UK: Department for Education and Skills.

Dillon, J., & Dickie, I. (2012). Learning in the natural environment: Review of social and economic benefits and barriers. *Natural England Commissioned Reports, 092*. London: Natural England.

Dillon, J., & Lovell, R. (2022). Links between natural environments, learning and health: Evidence briefing. *Natural England Evidence Information Note. EIN063*.

Dodd, H. F., Fitzgibbon, L., Watson, B. E., & Nesbit, R. J. (2021). Children's play and independent mobility in 2020: Results from the British children's play survey. School of Psychology and Clinical Language Sciences, University of Reading, Reading RG6 6ES, UK. *International Journal of Environmental Research and Public Health, 18*(8), 4334. https://doi.org/10.3390/ijerph18084334.

DoH. (1989). *Children Act*. Department of Health.

Dowdell, K., Gray, T., & Malone, K. (2010, 2011). Nature and its influence on children's outdoor play. *Australian Journal of Outdoor Education, 15*(2), 24–35.

Duckett, R., & Drummond, M. J. (2009). *Adventuring in Early Childhood Education*. Newcastle upon Tyne: Sightlines Initiative.

Early Education. (2015). *Achieving Excellence in the Early Years: A Guide for Headteachers*. London: BAECE.

Early Education Authors. (2015). *Achieving Excellence in the Early Years: A Guide for Headteachers*. London: BAECE.

Early Education Journal. (Autumn 2020). No. 92. In *Exploring the Wider World*. Editor: Caroline Eaton. Available at www.early-education.org.uk.

Early Years Coalition. (2021). *Birth to 5 Matters: Non-Statutory Guidance for the Early Years Foundation Stage*. St Albans: Early Education. Available at https://birthto5matters.org.uk/wp-content/uploads/2021/04/Birthto5Matters-download.pdf.

Early Years Foundation Stage. (2014). Birth to 5 Matters is published by Early Education on behalf of the Early Years Coalition, (2014).

Edwards, C. P. (1995). *Democratic Participation in a Community of Learners: Loris Malaguzzi's Philosophy of Education as Relationship* (p. 15). Faculty Publications, Department of Child, Youth and Family Studies.

Ellaway, A., Kirk, A., Macintyre, S., & Mutrie, N. (2007, June). Nowhere to play: The relationship between the location of outdoor play areas and deprivation in Glasgow. *Health and Place, 13*(2), 557–561.

Elliott, S., Arlemalm-Hagser, E., & Davis, J. (2020). *Researching Early Childhood Education for Sustainability: Challenging Assumptions and Orthodoxies*. Abingdon Routledge.

Elliott, S., & Davis, J. (2009). Exploring the resistance: An Australian perspective on educating for sustainability in early childhood. *International Journal of Early Childhood, 41*, 65–77.

Engdahl, I. (2015, September). Early childhood education for sustainability The OMEP world project. *International Journal of Early Childhood, 47*(3). https://doi.org/10.1007/s13158-015-0149-6.

Engelen, E., Wyver, S., Perry, G., Bundy, A., Kit Yee Chan, T., Ragen, J., Bauman, A., & Naughton, G. (2018). Spying on children during a school playground intervention using a novel method for direct observation of activities during outdoor play. *Journal of Adventure Education and Outdoor Learning, 18*(1), 86–95. https://doi.org/10.1080/14729679.2017.1347048.

Enoksen, E., & Lynch, P. (2017). Learning leadership: Becoming an outdoor leader. *Journal of Adventure Education and Outdoor Learning*. http://dx.doi.org/10.1080/14729679.2017.1391105.

Ernst, J. (2014). Early childhood educators' use of natural outdoor settings as learning environments: An exploratory study of beliefs, practices and barriers. *Environmental Education Research, 20*, 735–752.

Ewert, A., & Sibthorp, J. (2014). *Outdoor Adventure Education: Theory and Research*. Champaign, IL: Human Kinetics.

Fägerstam, E. (2012). Space and place: Perspectives of outdoor teaching and learning. PhD thesis. Linköping, Sweden: Linköping University. Available at http://liu.diva-portal.org/smash/get/diva2:551531/FULLTEXT01.pdf. Accessed 11 March 2017.

Fägerstam, E. (2014). High school teachers' experience of the educational potential of outdoor teaching and learning. *Journal of Adventure Education and Outdoor Learning, 14*(1), 56–81.

Field, F. (2010). *The Foundation Years: Preventing Poor Children Becoming Poor Adults: The Report of the Independent Review on Poverty and Life Chances*. London: The Cabinet Office.

Fiennes, C., Oliver, E., Dickson, K., Escobar, D., Romans, A., & Oliver, S. (2015). The existing evidence-base about effectiveness of outdoor learning. *Institute of Outdoor Learning, Blagrave Trust, UCL and Giving Evidence Report*.

Finney, C. (2014). *Black Faces, White Spaces: African Americans and the Great Outdoors*. Chapel Hill: UNC Press.

Fisher, J. (2016). *Interacting or Interfering? Improving Interactions in the Early Years*. Maidenhead: Open University Press.

Formosinho, J., & Oliviera-Formosinho, J. (2012). Praxeological Research in early childhood: a contribution to a social science of the social. *European Early Childhood Education Research Journal, 20*(4).

Frank Field The Foundation Years. (2010). The field report: Preventing poor children becoming poor adults. HM Government.

Fraser, S. (2007). Play in other language. *Theory into Practice, 46*(1), 14–22. http://dx.doi.org/10.1080/00405840709336544.

Freeman, C., & Tranter, P. (2011). *Children's Urban Environments: Changing Worlds*. Earthscan.

Freire, P. (1993). *Pedagogy of the Oppressed*. New York: Continuum.

Fröbel, F. (1887). The education of man. In D. N. Robinson (Ed.) *Significant Contributions to the History of Psychology 1750–1920*. University of Public of America.

Gaster, S. (1991). Urban children's access to their neighbourhoods: Changes over three generations. In Quoted in Louv, R. (2005). *Last Child in the Woods* (p. 123). Atlantic Books.

Gibson, J. J. (1979). *The ecological approach to visual perception*. Houghtom, Mifflin and Company.

Gilbert, J., & Knight, R. (2017). *Dirt Is Good: The Advantage of Germs for Your Child's Developing Immune System*. New York: St. Martin's Press.

Gill, T. (2004, September 20). Bred in captivity. *The Guardian*.

Gill, T. (2007). *No Fear*. UK: Calouste Gulbenkian Foundation.

Ginn, F., & Demeritt, D. (2010). Nature. In S. L. Holloway, S. P. Rice, G. Valentine, & N. Clifford (Eds.) *Key Concepts in Geography* (2nd ed.). London: Sage.

Goddard Blythe, S. (2004). *The Well-Balanced Child: Movement and Early Learning* ("Early Years"). Stroud: Hawthorn Press.

Goouch, K., & Powell, S. (2013). *The Baby Room: Principles, Policy and Practice*. Maidenhead, UK: Open University Press.

Gopnik, A., Meltzoff, A., & Kuhl, P. (1999). *How Babies Think: The Science of Childhood*. London: Weidenfeld and Nicolson.

Goswami, U. (2008). *Cognitive Development: The Learning Brain*. Psychology Press.

Graham Allen, M.P. (2011). Allen report: Early intervention: The next steps. Cabinet Office, HM Government.

Grahn, P., Martensson, F., Linblad, B., Nilsson, P., & Ekman, A. (1997). Outdoors in preschool. *Stad and Land, 145*, 96–97.

Gray, T., & Mitten, D. (2018). *The Palgrave International Handbook of Women and Outdoor Learning*. London: Palgrave Macmillan.

Greenland, P. (2010). Physical development. In T. Bruce (Ed.) *Early Childhood: A Guide for Students* (pp. 188–192). London: Sage.

Gull, C., Levenson Goldstein, S., & Rosengarten, T. (2020). Early childhood educators' perspectives on tree climbing. *International Journal of Early Childhood Environmental Education, 8*(1), 26–43. Available at naturalstart.org

Gullestad, M. (1997). A Passion for boundaries – reflections on connections between the everyday lives of children and discourses on the nation in contemporary Norway. *Childhood, 4*(1), 19–42. https://doi.org/10.1177/0907568297004001002.

Gussin Payley, V. (1986). On listening to what the children say. *Harvard Education Review, 77*(2), 152–163.

Hadley, F. (2012). Early childhood staff and families' perceptions: Diverse views about important experiences for children aged 3–5 years in early childhood settings. *Contemporary Issues in Early Childhood, 13*(1), 38–48.

The Hadow Report. (1933). *Report of the Consultative Committee on Infant and Nursery Schools*. London: Her Majesty's Stationery Office.

Harries, A., & Jones, M. (2015). *Leading Futures: Global Perspectives on Educational Leadership*. Sage Department for Education.

Hart, R. A. (1995a). Affection for nature and the promotion of earth stewardship in childhood. *The NAMTA Journal, 2*(20), 59–68.

Harwood, D. (2019). The blue car in the forest: Exploring children's experiences of sustainability in a Canadian Forest. *NORDINA, 15*(4), 403–4 7.

Hayes, N., O'Toole, L., & Halpenny, A. (2017). *Introducing Bronfenbrenner: A Guide for Practitioners and Students in Early Years Education*. Abingdon: Routledge.

Henderson, B., & Vikancler, N. (eds.). (2007). *Nature First: Outdoor Ljfe the Friltdfsliv Way*. Ontario, Canada: Natural Heritage Books. Find out more *a outfl'ihcftsliv*.

Hughes, A. (2016). *Developing Play for the Under 3's* (3rd ed.). Abingdon: Routledge.

Hunt, A., Stewart, D., Burt, J., & Dillon, J. (2016). Monitor of engagement with the natural environment: A pilot to develop an indicator of visits to the natural environment by children. *Gov.uk*. Available at assets.publishing.service.gov.uk.

International School Grounds Alliance. (2017). *Risk in Play and Learning: Ubud-Hoor Declaration*. Available at www.internationalschoolgrounds.org/risk.

Isaacs, S. (1930). *Intellectual Growth in Young Children*. London: Routledge and Kegan Paul.

Isaacs, S. (1954). *The Educational Value of the Nursery School*. London: The Nursery School Association.

Jackson, K. (2015). *A Practical Guide – Outdoor Learning*. Woodbridge: John Catt.

James, C., & Chakraborty, S. *COVID-19 Is a Precursor for Infectious Disease Outbreaks on a Warming Planet*. Available at http://thehill.com/opinion/healthcare/534562-covid-19-is-a-precursor-for-the-infectious-disease-outbreaks-in-a-warming. Accessed 20 August 2021.

Jarvis, P. (2006). Rough and tumble play: Lessons in life. *Evolutionary Psychology, 4*, 330–346.

Jarvis, P., & Liebovich, B. (2015). British nurseries, head and heart: McMillan, owen and the genesis of the education/care dichotomy. *Women's History Review, 24*(6), 917–937. https://doi.org/10.1080/09612025.2015.1025662.

Jayasuriya, A., Williams, M., Edwards, T., & Tandon, P. (2016). Parents' perceptions of preschool activities: Exploring outdoor play. *Early Education and Development, 27*, 1004–1017. https://doi.org/10.1080/10409289.2016.1156989. [Taylor & Francis Online], [Web of Science ®], [Google Scholar].

Jenkins, E. W. (2000). The impact of the national curriculum on secondary school science teaching in England and Wales. *International Journal of Science Education, 22*(3), 325–336.

Kahn, Jr., P. H., & Kellert, S. R. (2002). *Children and Nature: Psychological, Sociocultural, and Evolutionary Investigations*. Cambridge, MA: MIT Press.

Kane, A., & Kane, J. (2011). Waldkindergarten in Germany. *Green Teacher, 94*, 16–19.

Kaser, L., & Halbert, J. (2009). *Leadership Mindsets: Innovation and Learning in the Transformation of Schools*. London: Routledge.

Katz, L. (1995). *Talks with Teachers of Young Children*. New Jersey: Ablex Publishing Company.

Katz, L. (2010). *STEM in the Early Years*. Urbana and Champaign: University of Illinois.

Kemp, N. (2020). Views from the staffroom: Forest school in English primary schools. *Journal of Adventure Education & Outdoor Learning, 20*(4), 369–380.

Kemp, N., & Josephidou, J. (2021). Babies and toddlers outdoors: A narrative review of the literature on provision for under twos in ECEC settings. *Early Years*. https://doi.org/10.1080/09575146.2021.1915962.

Kernan, M., & Devine, D. (2010, September). Being confined within? Constructions of the good childhood and outdoor play in early childhood education and care settings in Ireland. *Children & Society, 24*(5), 371–385.

Kleppe, R. (2018, May). One-to-three-year-olds' risky play in early childhood education and care. Thesis.

Kranowitz, C. S. (2005). *The Out-of-Sync Child: Recognizing and Coping with Sensory Processing Disorder*. New York: A Skylight Press Book/A Perigee Book.

Kuh, L., Ponte, I., & Chau, C. (2013). The impact of a natural playscape installation on young children's play behaviours. *Children, Youth and Environments, 23*. https://doi.org/10.7721/chilyoutenvi.23.2.0049.

Kutnick, P., Brighi, A., Avgitidou, S., Genta, M. L., Hännikäinen, M., Karlsson-Lohmander, M., & Lofqvist, M. (2007). The role and practice of interpersonal relationships in European early education settings: Sites for enhancing social inclusion, personal growth and learning? *European Early Childhood Education Research Journal, 15*(3), 379–406. https://doi.org/10.1080/13502930701679429.

Laevers, F. (1993). Deep level learning: An exemplary application on the area of physical knowledge. *European Early Childhood Research Journal*, *1*(1), 53–68.

Laevers, F. (1997). Assessing the quality of childcare provision: "Involvement" as criterion. *Researching Early Childhood*, *3*, 151–165.

Laevers, F. (2005). *Deep-Level-Learning and the Experiential Approach in Early Childhood and Primary Education*. Leuven: Katholieke Universiteit Leuvan Research Centre for Early Childhood and Primary Education.

Leithwood, K., Jantzi, D., & McElheron-Hopkins, C. (2006). The development and testing of a school improvement model. *School Effectiveness and School Improvement*, *17*(4), 441–464. https://doi.org/10.1080/09243450600743533.

Lester, S., & Maudslesy, M. (2007). *Play, Naturally*. London: NCB.

Little, H. (2006). Children's risk-taking behaviour: Implications for early childhood policy and practice. *International Journal of Early Years Education*, *14*(2), 141–154.

Louv, R. (2005/2008). *Last Child in the Woods: Saving Our Children from Nature-Deficit Disorder*. Chapel Hill: Algonquin Books.

Lysklett, O. B., Emilsen, K., & Hagen, T. L. (2003). What characterizes the nature in outdoor nursery? *Kindergarten People Pedagogic Forum*, [illegible], 78–85.

MacDonald, K. (1987). Parent-child physical play with rejected, neglected and popular boys. *Developmental Psychology*, *23*, 705–711.

Macfarlane, R., & Morris, J. (2017). *The Lost Words*. Italy: Hamish Hamilton/Penguin Random House.

Macfarlane, R., & Morris, J. (2020). *The Lost Spells*. Italy: Hamish Hamilton/Penguin Random House.

Macintyre, F. (2009). A longitudinal examination of the contribution of perceived motor competence and actual motor competence to physical activity in 6 to 9-year-old children. Doctor of Philosophy, The University of Notre Dame, Australia.

Macnab, D. S. (2003). Implementing change in mathematics education. *Journal of Curriculum Studies*, *35*, 197–215.

Marmot, M. (2010). *Fair Society, Healthy Lives: Equity from the Start*. London: UCL, Institute of Health Equity.

Marshall, J. (1984). *Women Managers: Travellers in a Male World*. Chichester, UK & New York, USA.

Mårtensson, F. (2004). *Landskapet i leken – En studie av utomhuslek på förskolegården* (p. 464). Alnarp: Agraria.

Martin, B., Cashel, C., Wagstaff, M., & Breunig, M. (2006). *Outdoor Leadership: Theory and Practice*. Champaign, IL: Human Kinetics.

Mathieson, K. (2013). *I Am Two! Working Effectively with to-Year-Olds and Their Families*. London: The British Association for Early Childhood Education.

Maynard, T. (2007). A risky business? Encounters with forest school and Foucault. *Education 3–13*, 379–391.

Maynard, T., & Chicken, S. (2010). Through a different lens: Exploring Reggio Emilia in a Welsh context. *Early Years: An International Journal of Research and Development*, *30*(1), 29–39.

Maynard, T., & Waters, J. (2007). Learning in the outdoor environment: A missed opportunity. *Early Years: An International Journal of Research and Development*, *27*(3), 255–265.

McClintic, S., & Petty, K. (2015, February 3). Exploring early childhood teachers' beliefs and practices about preschool outdoor play: A qualitative study. *Journal of Early Childhood Teacher Education, 36*. https://doi.org/10.1080/10901027.2014.997844.

McClure, E. (2017, November). More than a foundation: Young children are capable STEM learners. *Young Children, 72*(5), 83–89.

McCree, M. Cutting, R., & Sherwin, D. (2018). The hare and the tortoise go to forest school: Taking the scenic route to academic attainment via emotional wellbeing outdoors. *Early Child Development and Care, 188*(7), 980–996. https://doi.org/10.1080/03004430.2018.1446430.

McDowall, C., & Murray, J. (2012). *Reconceptualizing Leadership in the Early Years.* Maidenhead: Open University Press.

McInnes, K., Howard, J., Miles, G., & Crowley, K. (2011). Differences in practitioners' understanding of play and how this influences pedagogy and children's perceptions of play. *Early Years, 31*, 121–133.

McMillan, M. (1919). *The Nursery School.* London: J.M. Dent & Sons Ltd.

Merewether, J. (2019a) Listening with young children: Enchanted animism of trees, rocks, clouds (and other things). *Pedagogy, Culture and Society, 27*(2), 233–250.

Morrissey, A. M., Scott, C., & Wishart, L. (2015). Infant and toddler responses to a redesign of their childcare outdoor play space. *Children, Youth and Environments, 25.* https://doi.org/10.7721/chilyoutenvi.25.1.0029.

Moyles, J. (2001). Passion, paradox and professionalism in early years education. *Early Years, 21*(2), 81–95. https://doi.org/10.1080/09575140124792.

Mullan, K. (2018). A child's day: Trends in time use in the UK from 1975 to 2015. https://doi.org/10.1111/1468-4446.12369.

Murray, L. (2014). *The Psychology of Babies: How Relationships Support Development from Birth to Two.* London: Constable & Robinson.

Natural England Report. (2013). Engaging children on the autistic spectrum with the natural environment: Teacher insight study and evidence review. *Access to Nature Final Evaluation Report Part 2: Inspiring People to Engage with Their Natural Environment*, PDF, 4.3 M.

Natural England. (2016a). *England's Largest Outdoor Learning Project Reveals Children More Motivated to Learn When Outside* [Online]. Available at www.gov.uk/government/news/englands-largest-outdoor-learning-project-reveals-children-more-motivated-to-learn-when-outside. Accessed 21 January 2017.

Natural England. (2016b). *Natural Connections Demonstration Project 2012–2016 Final Report.* NECR215 Publications. Available at naturalengland.org.uk/publication/6636651036540928 www.google.com/search?q=The+National+Trust+research+%E2%80%9CNatural+Childhood%E2%80%9D+%282016%29+&client=safari&rls=en&ei=Tr0PYeyHK4OC8gLVnbKABQ&oq=The+National+Trust+research+%E2%80%9CNatural+Childhood%E2%80%9D+%282016%29+&gs_lcp=Cgdnd3Mtd2l6EAMyBQghEKABMgUIIRCgATIFCCEQoAEyBQghEKABMgUIIRCgAUoECEEYAFD-EljZJ2CdNmgBcAB4AIABYIgBYJIBATGYAQCgAQGgAQKwAQDAAQE&sclient=gws-wiz&ved=0ahUKEwjs5ujSpqHyAhUDgVwKHdWODFAQ4dUDCA4&uact=5.

Natural England: Social Value Business. (2022). *Social & Economic Benefits of Learning in Natural Environments: A Study of Learning Outside the Classroom in Natural*

Environments (LINE) in Primary School Settings to Provide a Forecast of Social Value. NECR442. Natural England.

Neblong, H. (1999). *Keynote to the Design on Play Conference.* Available at www.deepfun.com/2002/12/helle-nebelong-on-designing-playspaces.html.

Nedovic, S., & Morrissey, A. M. (2013). Calm active and focused: Children's responses to an organic outdoor learning environment. *Learning Environments Research, 16.* https://doi.org/10.1007/s10984-013-9127-9.

Neil, J. (2007, May 1). History of outdoor education. *Wilderdom.com.* Available at www.wilderdom.com/History.html. Accessed 29 September 2014.

Nelson, E. M. (2012). *Cultivating Outdoor Classrooms: Designing and Implementing Child-Centered Learning Environments.* St. Paul, MN: Redleaf Print.

Nesbit, R. J., Bagnall, C. L., Harvey, K., & Dodd, H. F. (2021). Perceived barriers and facilitators of adventurous play in schools: A qualitative systematic review. *Children, 8*(8), 681. https://doi.org/10.3390/children8080681.

NHS Digital. (2019.) *National Child Measurement Programme England, 2018/19 School Year.* Available at https://files.digital.nhs.uk/33/A1D2CB/nati-chil-meas-prog-eng-2018-2019-app.pdf.

Nicholson, J., Shimpi, P., Kunik, J., Carducci, C., & Jevgjovikj, M. (2014). Listening to children's perspectives on play across the lifespan: Children's right to inform adults' discussions of contemporary play. *International Journal of Play, 3,* 136–156.

Nicholson, S. (1971). How not to cheat children: Theory of loose parts. In *Landscape Architecture* (Vol. 62, pp. 30–34). Harrisburg, PA and Chapel Hill, NC: Algonquin Books.

NI Direct Government Services. *Playing Outdoors Briefing Sheet 2.* Available at Playmatters@education-ni.gov.uk. Accessed March 2024.

Nilsen, R. D. (2008). Children in nature: Cultural ideas and social practices in Norway. In A. James & A. L. James (Eds.) *European Childhoods: Cultures, Politics and Childhoods.* Basingstoke: Palgrave.

Nutbrown, C. (2006). *Threads of Thinking: Young Children Learning and the Role of Early Education* (3rd ed.). London: Sage.

Nye, D. (2001). in conversation with Kathryn Solly.

Oberle, E., Zeni, M., Munday, F., & Brussoni, M. (2021). Support factors and barriers for outdoor learning in elementary schools: A systemic perspective. *American Journal of Health Education.* https://doi.org/10.1080/19325037.2021.1955232.

O'Brien, L., & Murray, R. (2007, November 15). Forest school and its impacts on young children: Case studies in britain. *Urban Forestry and Urban Greening, 6*(4), 249–265.

OFSTED. (2015). *Teaching and Play in the Early Years – a Balancing Act?* Available at www.gov.uk/government/organisations/ofsted.

OFSTED. (2017). *Bold Beginnings: The Reception Curriculum in a Sample of Good and Outstanding Primary Schools.* Available at www.gov.uk/ofsted.

O'Haire, M, E. (2013). Animal-assisted intervention for autism spectrum disorder: A systematic literature review. *Journal of Autism and Developmental Disorders, 43,* 1606–1622.

Osborn, M. (2003). *A World of Difference?: Comparing Learners across Europe.* Buckingham: Open University Press.

Osgood, J. (2010). Reconstructing professionalism in ECEC: The case for the 'critically reflective emotional professional'. *Early Years: An International Journal of Research and Development, 30*(2), 119–133.

Ouvry, M. (2003). *Exercising Muscles and Minds: Outdoor Play and the Early Years Curriculum.* NCB.

Palaiologou, I. (ed.). (2012). *The Early Years Foundation Stage.* London: Sage.

Pansardi, P., & Bindi, M. (2021). The new concepts of power? Power-over. Power-to and power-with. *Journal of Political Power, 14*(1), 51–71.

Paquette, D., Carbonneau, R., Debeau, D., Bigras, M., & Tremplay, R. E. (2003). Prevalence of father child rough and tumble play and physical aggression in pre-school children. *European Journal of Psychology of Education, 18*, 171–189.

Pasch, J. (2014). *Engaging Two Year Olds Through Fun and Creative Play: What Children need to Do.* Newham: Early Education.

Peckham, K. (2017). *Developing School Readiness.* London: Sage.

Pelo, A. (2013). *The Goodness of Rain: Developing an Ecological Identity in Young Children.* Redmond: Exchange Press.

Penetito, W. (2009). Place-based education: Catering for curriculum, culture and community. *The New Zealand Annual Review of Education, 18*(18), 5–29.

Perrin, J. M., Bloom, S. R., & Gortmaker, S. L. (2007). The increase of childhood chronic conditions in the United States. *JAMA, 297*(24), 2755–2759.

Pramling Samuelsson, I., & Kaga, Y. (2015). ED.2008/WS/14. UNESCO Digital Library.

Prescott, E. (1987). The environment as organizer of intent in child-care settings. In C. S. Weinstein & T. G. David (Eds.) *Spaces for Children: The Built Environment and Child Development* (Vol 9(1)). Early Childhood News.

Priest, S., & Gass, M. A. (1997). The range of teaching styles in adventure programming. *The Journal of Adventure Education and Outdoor Leadership, 14*(4), 12–14.

Priest, S., & Gass, M. A. (2005). *Effective Leadership in Adventure Programming.* Champaign, IL: Human Kinetics.

Pryor, A., Carpenter, C., & Townsend, M. (2015). Outdoor education and bush adventure therapy: A socio-ecological approach to health and wellbeing. *Australian Journal of Outdoor Education, 9*(1), 3–13.

Read, J. (1992). A short history of children's building blocks. In P. Gura (Ed.) *Exploring Learning: Young Children and Blockplay* (pp. 1–12). London: Paul Chapman.

Rickinson, M., Hunt, A., Rogers, J., & Dillon, J. (2012). *School Leader and Teacher Insights into Learning Outside the Classroom in Natural Environments.* London: Natural England.

Robb, M., Mew, V., & Richardson, A. (2015). *Learning with Nature.* Cambridge: Green Books.

Robertson, J. (2014). *Dirty Teaching.* Carmarthen: Independent Thinking Press.

Robertson, J. (2017). *Messy Maths.* Bloomsbury: Crown House.

Robottom, I. (ed.). (1987). *Environmental Education: Practice and Possibility.* Geelong, VIC: Deakin University Press. (2007, April). *Environmental Education Research, 13*(2), 139–153. New York, USA: University at Buffalo.

Rodd, J. (2001). Building leadership expertise of future early childhood professionals. *Journal of Early Childhood Teacher Education, 22*(1), 9–12. https://doi.org/10.1080/10901027.2001.10486430. Downloaded from search.informit.org/doi/10.3316/

informit.804638988383910. on 08/04/2021 01:15 AM AEST; UTC+10:00. © Journal of Educational Leadership, Policy and Practice, 2018.

Rodd, J. (2006). *Leadership in Early Childhood* (3rd ed.). Maidenhead: Open University Press.

Rodd, J. (2015). *Leading Change in the Early Years.* Maidenhead, Berkshire: McGraw Hill Education.

Rogers, A., & Smith, M. K. (2012). *Learning through Outdoor Experience: A Guide for Schools and Youth Groups* (pp. 1–8). Canning Town, London: YMCA George Williams College for the Rank Foundation. Accessed 29 September 2014.

Rogoff, B. (1994). *Mind, Culture and Activity.* Abingdon: Taylor and Francis.

Rosen, M. (2010). Foreward. In C. Tims (Ed.) *Born Creative.* Available at www.demos.co.uk/project/born-creative/.

Rouse. E. 2015. Making learning visible – parents perceptions of children's learning outdoors. *Early Child Development and Care, 186*(4), 612–623. [Taylor & Francis Online].

Ryder, D., Chandra, Y., Dalton, J., Homer, M., & Passingham, D. (2011). The development process of an early childhood leadership programme: A distributive leadership perspective. New Zealand College of Early Childhood Education. *Journal of Educational Leadership, Policy and Practice, 26*(2), 62–68.

Şad, S., & Gurbuzturk, O. (2013). Primary school students' parents' keve_ of involvement into their children's education. *Educational Sciences: Theory and Practice, 13*(2), 1006–1011. [Google Scholar].

Sandseter, E. B. H. (2009a). Affordances for risky play in preschool: The importance of features in the play environment. *Early Childhood Education Journal, 36*(5), 439–446. https://doi.org/10.1007/s10643-009-0307-2.

Sandseter, E. B. H. (2009b). Characteristics of risky play. *Journal of Adventure Education & Outdoor Learning, 9*(1), 3–21. https://doi.org/10.1080/14729670802702762.

Sandseter, E. B. H. (2009c). Risky play and risk management in Norwegian preschools – a qualitative observational study. *Safety Science Monitor, 13*, 1–12.

Sandseter, E. B. H., & Sando, O. J. (2016). We don't allow children to climb trees: How a focus on safety affects norwegian children's play in early-childhood education and care settings. *American Journal of Play, 8.*

Schnack, K. (2008). Participation, education, and democracy: Implications for environmental education, health education, and education for sustainable development. In A. Reid, B. B. Jensen, J. Nikel, & V. Simovska (Eds.) *Participation and Learning: Perspectives on Education and the Environment, Health and Sustainability* (pp. 181–196). Netherland: Springer.

Scrutton, R., & Beames, S. (2015). Measuring the unmeasurable: Upholding rigor in quantitative studies of personal and social development in outdoor adventure education. *Journal of Experiential Education, 38*(1), 8–25.

Shooter, W., Sibthorp, J., & Paisley, K. (2009). The social system in outdoor adventure education. *Journal of Experiential Education, 32*, 1–13.

Southworth, G. (1998). *Leading Improving Primary Schools: The Work of Headteachers and Deputy Heads.* London: Falmer Press.

Southworth, G. (1999). Primary school leadership: Policy, practice and theory. *School Leadership and Management, 19*(1), 49–65.

Southworth, G. (2002a). Instructional leadership in schools: Reflections and empirical evidence. *School Leadership and Management, 22*(1), 73–91.

Southworth, G. (2002b). Lessons from successful small school leadership. In K. Leithwood, P. Hallinger, G. Furman-Brown, B. Mulford, P. Gronn, K. Riley, & K. Seashore Louis (Eds.) *Second International Handbook of Educational Leadership and Administration*. Norwell, MA: Kluwer Academic Press.

Scottish Government. (2019). *Raising the Ambition*. Available at https://education.gov.scot/improvement/learningresources/realising-the-ambition/.

Scottish Government. (2020, February 10). *Out to Play-Creating Outdoor Play Experiences for Children: Practical Guidance*. Early Learning and Childcare Directorate. ISBN: 9781787814448.

Sobel, D. (2008). *Childhood and Nature: Design Principles for Educators*. Portland, ME: Stenhouse.

Sobel, D. (2012, July–August). Look, don't touch the problem with environmental education. *Orion Magazine*. Available at www.orionmagazine.org/index.php/articles/article/6929.

Sobel, D. (2013a). *Beyond Ecophobia: Reclaiming the Heart in Nature Education*. Great Barrington, MA: Orion Society.

Sobel, D. (2013b). *Place-Based Education: Connecting Classrooms and Communities*. Great Barrington, MA: Orion.

Sobel, D. (2016). *Nature Preschools and Forest Kindergartens: The Handbook for Outdoor Learning*. St. Paul, MN: Redleaf Press.

Sobel, D. (2019). *Beyond Ecophobia: Reclaiming the Heart of Nature Education*. Orion Reader.

Spillane, J. P. (2005). Distributed leadership. *The Educational Forum*, *69*(2), 143–150. https://doi.org/10.1080/00131720508984678.

Spillane, J. P., Halverson, R., & Diamond, J. B. (2001). Investigating school leadership practice: A distributed perspective. *Educational Researcher*, *30*(3), 23–28. Available at www.jstor.org.

Stan, I. (2010). Control as an educational tool and its impact on the outdoor educational process. *Australian Journal of Outdoor Education*, *14*(2), 12–20.

Stevenson, H. (2007). Restructuring teachers' work and trade union responses in England: Bargaining for change. *American Education Research Journal*, *44*(2), 224–251.

Stevenson, K. (2007). *Educational Trends Shaping School Planning and Design: 2007*. Washington, DC: National Clearinghouse for Educational Facilities.

Stevenson, R. B. (1987 [2007]). Schooling and environmental education: Contradictions in purpose and practice. *Environmental Education Research*, *13*(2), 139–153.

Stonehouse, A. (2011). *The More You Know, the More You See: Babies' and Toddlers' Learning and the EYLF*. Deakin West, ACT: Early Childhood Australia.

Sutton Trust Report. (2014). *What Makes Great Teaching?* Available at www.suttontrust.com/wp-content/uploads/2014/10/What-Makes-Great-Teaching-REPORT.pdf.

Sylva, K. (2004). *The Effective Pre-School Project EPPE Project*. Available at https://dera.ioe.ac.uk/18189/2/SSU-SF-2004-01.pdf.

Szczpanski, A. (red.). (2007). *Outdoor Education as a Source of Information – the Local Environment as a Source of Knowledge*. Lund: Studentlitteratur.

Tassoni, P. (2016). *Reducing Educational Disadvantage*. London: Bloomsbury.

Te-Whariki Early Childhood Curriculum. (2017). *Ministry of Education*, New Zealand. ISBN 978-0-478-16927-0 (Online).

Tiplady, L. S. E., & Harriet Menter, H. (2021). Forest school for wellbeing: An environment in which young people can "take what they need". *Journal of Adventure Education & Outdoor Learning*, *21*(2), 99–114.

Tovey, H. (2007). *Playing Outdoors: Spaces and Places, Risks and Challenges*. Berkshire, England: McGraw-Hill, Open University Press.

Tovey, H. (2013). *Bringing the Froebel Approach to your Early Years Practice*. London: Routledge.

Tsing, A. L. (2013). More than human sociality: A call for critical description. In K. Hastrup (Ed.) *Anthropology and Nature* (pp. 27–42). New York: Routledge.

Twohig-Bennett, C., & Jones, A. (2018). The health benefits of the great outdoors: A systematic review and meta-analysis of greenspace exposure and health outcomes. *Environmental Research Journal*, *166*, 628–637.

Uhl-Bien, M. (2006). Relational leadership theory: Exploring the social processes of leadership and organizing. *The Leadership Quarterly*, *17*(6), 654–676. https://doi.org/10.1016/j.leaqua.2006.10.007.

UNESCO. (2008). *The Contribution of Early Childhood Education to a Sustainable Society*. Available at https://unesdoc.unesco.org/images/0015/001593/159355E.pdf. Accessed 25 August 2015.

Waite, S. (ed.). (2011). *Children Learning Outside the Classroom: From Birth to Eleven*. London: SAGE Publications.

Waller, T., Sandseter, E. B. H., Wyver, S., Ärlemalm-Hagsér, E., & Maynard, T. (2010). The dynamics of early childhood spaces: Opportunities for outdoor play? *European Early Childhood Research Journal*, *8*. https://doi.org/10.1080/1350293X.2010.525917.

Wandersee, J. H, & Schussler, E. E. (1999, February). Preventing plant blindness. *The American Biology Teacher*, *61*(2), 82+84+86 (3 pages), Published By: University of California Press.

Warden, C. (2010). *Nature Kindergartens*. UK: Mindstretchers, Ltd.

Warden, C. (2015). *Learning with Nature – Embedding Outdoor Practice*. London: Sage.

Warren, K., Mitten, D., D'Amore, C., & Lotz, E. (2018). The gendered hidden curriculum of adventure education. *The Journal of Experimental Education*, *42*(2), 140–154.

Watts, A. (2013). *Outdoor Learning through the Seasons*. Abingdon: Routledge.

Wells, G. (1986). *The Meaning Makers*. Portsmouth, USA: Heinemann.

Wells, G. (1987). *The Meaning Makers*. London: Hodder & Stoughton.

Whalley, M. (2005). *Developing Leadership Approaches for Early Years Settings*. Unpublished lecture at Pen Green.

Whalley, M., John, K., Whitaker, P., Klavins, E., Parker, C., & Vaggers, J. (2019). *Democratising Leadership in the Early Years-a Systemic Approach*. Abingdon: Routledge.

White, J. (2011). *Outdoor Provision in the Early Years: A Guide for Practitioners*. Edited by Jan White. Thousand Oaks, CA: Paul Chapman Publishing.

White, J. (2014a). *Playing and Learning Outdoors: Making Provision for High Quality Experiences in the Outdoor Environment with Children 3–7*. Abingdon, Oxon: Routledge.

White, J. (2014b). Ecological identity – values, principles and practice. In R. Duckett & M. J. Drummond (Eds.) *Learning to Learn in Nature*. Newcastle-upon-Tyne: Sightlines Initiative.

White, J. (2015). *Every Child a Mover*. London: The British Association for Early Childhood Education.

White, J. (2019). *Playing and Learning Outdoors – the Practical Guide and Sourcebook for Excellence in Outdoor Provision and Practice with Young Children* (3rd ed.). Abingdon: Routledge.

White, J., & Woolley, H. (2014). What makes a good outdoor environment for young children? In T. Maynard & J. Waters (Eds.) *Exploring Play in the Early Years*. Berkshire: Open University Press.

Whitebread, D., & Bingham, S. (2014). School readiness, starting age, cohorts and transitions in the early years. In J. Moyles, J. Payler, & J. Georgeson (Eds.) *Early Years Foundations: Critical Issues* (2nd ed., pp. 179–190). Maidenhead: Open University Press.

Whitebread, D., Kuvalja, M., & Verma, M. (2012, January). The importance of play: A report on the value of children's play with a series of policy recommendations. *Toy Industries of Europe Report*.

Whitebread, D., Neale, D., & Jensen, H. (2017). *The Role of Play in Children's Development: A Review of the Evidence*. The Lego Foundation. ResearchGate.

Wilson, E. O. (1984). *Biophilia*. Cambridge, MA: Harvard University Press.

Wilson, E. O. (1992). *The Diversity of Life*. Cambridge, MA: Harvard University Press.

Wilson, R. (2010). Goodness of fit: Good for children and good for the Earth. In J. L. Hoot & J. Szente (Eds.) *The Earth Is Our Home* (pp. 17–35). Olney, MD: Association for Childhood Education International.

Wilson, R. (2012). *Nature and Young Children* (2nd ed.). New York and Abingdon: Routledge.

Woods, A. (2017). *Elemental Play and Outdoor Learning*. Abingdon: Routledge.

Wurm, J. (2005). MN.ERIC No. ED564307. St. Paul: Redleaf Press.

Wyver, S., Tranter, P., Naughton, G., Little, H., Sandseter, E. B. H., & Bundy, A. (2010, January 1). Ten ways to restrict children's freedom to play: The problem of surplus safety. *Research Article in Contemporary Issues in Early Education*. https://doi.org/10.2304/ciec.2010.11.3.263.

Zosh, J., Hopkins, E., Jensen, H., Liu, C., Neale, D., Hirsh-Pasek, K., Solis, L., & Whitebread, D. M. (2017, November). White Paper. Learning through Play: A review of the evidence. The Lego Foundation, DK. Licensed under a Creative Commons Attribution-NonCommercial-ShareAlike 3.0 Unported License. https://doi.org/10.13140/RG.2.2.16823.01447.

Index

Note: Page numbers in *italics* indicate figures

www.ingramcontent.com/pod-product-compliance
Lightning Source LLC
LaVergne TN
LVHW081324110826
845149LV00007B/1585

* 9 7 8 1 1 3 8 3 4 8 8 5 1 *